FUTURE-FOCUSED

SHAPE YOUR

CULTURE

SHAPE YOUR

FUTURE

ROSE GAILEY & IAN JOHNSTON

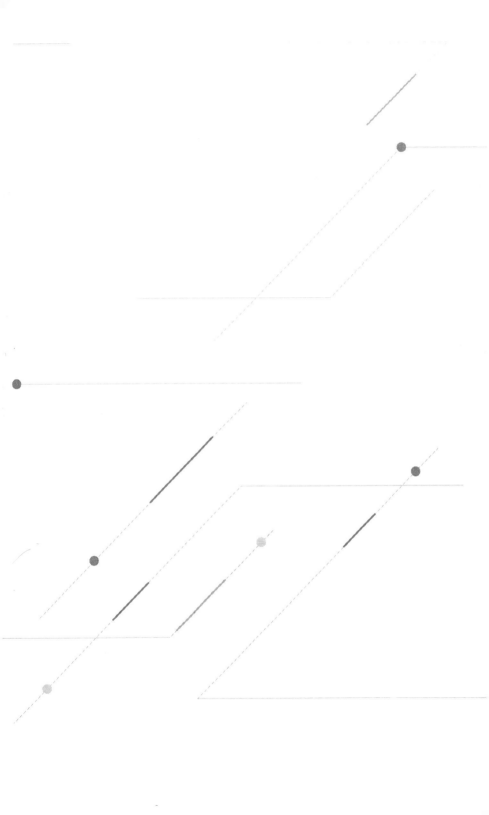

We dedicate this book to our clients, who are committed to building thriving cultures and organizations. Their leadership shadows make the world a better place.

We also dedicate this book to our colleagues at Heidrick & Struggles. Together, we are passionate about enabling a world better led.

Table of contents

Foreword:
Why culture?

Krishnan
Rajagopalan

**President & CEO,
Heidrick & Struggles**

Heidrick & Struggles was founded as an executive search firm, and for a long time we thrived with that sole focus. But of course some leaders didn't succeed in their roles, and when we talked with leaders and clients about why, it often came down to a vague discussion about "fit." Nobody talked about—and few people knew—what that really meant.

It means culture impact: how leaders influence an organization's culture, positively or negatively.

We began to acknowledge the importance of thinking in a serious, formalized way about how someone would affect an organization's culture—and how that would affect both their individual success and the organization's success. When we acquired Senn Delaney in 2013, we built on their proven methodology of putting the right language around culture, being able to measure it and assess how individuals' capabilities and experiences would or would not align with it. Since then, we have seen the benefit to organizations' performance of being able to have an informed dialogue on this topic as we help companies and leaders.

And today, culture matters more than ever. It's already clear that culture is going to be one of biggest influences on team performance as working hybrid or remote becomes the post-pandemic norm. People are likely to feel less connected to their company and to each other. As leaders, we have to be sure there's some glue that brings things back together, and that glue is culture, starting with the underlying values, mission, and purpose that build connection and commitment.

Values and mission, coalesced into a socially meaningful purpose, were the crucial core of cultures that helped companies thrive before the pandemic and became even more important during it, as my colleagues Rose Gailey and Ian Johnston discuss in chapter 1. Going forward, leaders are going to have to focus even more sharply on a few important themes that people, communities, and society care passionately about. Diversity, equity, and inclusion (DE&I) is at the top of the list for many leaders. What does fair look like? How does a company begin to show it? Another is sustainability: what is our point of view as an organization on that and what steps are we willing to take to address it? To me, how the culture of an organization supports progress in these areas is going to be critical to whether people align with an organization. So culture is going to be very important as a vehicle for enhancing a team's performance, bringing people together. The stories in this book about Anthem, the health benefits service company, Lumen, the telecoms company, and Jack in the Box are all exemplars of how this works.

We also know that when leaders align culture and strategy, culture becomes an even more powerful performance accelerant. I have seen this in my own work, and a recent survey we conducted of CEOs around the world that is discussed throughout this book shows the same. When everyone is aligned on and inspired by a mission that is not only inclusive and socially meaningful but also linked to the company's value creation strategy, it's inspirational. And boom, you have performance. The stories in this book of Southwest Airlines, Yum! Brands, and DBS, the Singapore bank, highlight the power of such links. I really think it's about as simple as that. Aligning a thriving culture with strategy is how companies and CEOs can ensure they can generate sustained strong performance.

The reason is that culture is how we as leaders and organizations can address many of the barriers to executing strategy, whatever they might be. One example is increasing diversity. Almost every company has been working on it at some level for at least 15 years. However, we haven't made a lot of progress. When we dig deeper into why companies can work on something for so long, with good intentions, and not get far, we get to underlying factors like behaviors and norms: culture. Understanding that gives leaders a new set of questions to ask and tools to use to make progress. And culture affects all areas of operations, anything that people do in a company: customer experience, safety, compliance, and innovation, to name just a few more.

Here at Heidrick & Struggles, for example, we've shaped our culture to bolster collaboration, which is an important tenet of our strategy. We are a leadership advisory firm, and we are transforming our business model to be able to bring the best solutions to our clients from anywhere in our organization, which requires a heightened level of collaboration. In our case, the good part of our various operational silos is that we have solutions coming from many sources, search and leadership development, for example, or organizational design. The challenging part is that we weren't all working in the same way, using the same language or metrics, for example. For the longest time, we wanted to collaborate, and people were working hard at it, but, we weren't getting far enough. It became clear to me that if we didn't come together as one team and enable ourselves to talk about performance in a very normal, tactical, and unified way together we probably wouldn't be able to collaborate and move forward. We had to think about having the right culture in place to be able to do that easily, and promote that culture. The story of Helen of Troy in chapter 7 is another example of the power of aligning financial and culture metrics.

Organizations and leaders that really want to move the dial on the bigger topics they're trying to address are going to have to get to those underlying issues, and they're going to have to fix mindsets and behaviors and how people come together in order to be able to advance. Those things are hard, and they take time.

CEOs have to make those investments, starting now. Given where the world is, and what's important to all our stakeholders, leaders who don't get started now on addressing whatever issues are in the way of their sustainable performance will start to go backwards. I don't think there's a choice.

For CEOs, I'd note that a thriving culture starts with us. Larry Senn pioneered the codification of organizational culture, including the concept of the "shadow of the leader," and I have seen it at work, for better and for worse. As CEO, I'm the chief architect of culture, and the person who others look to each and every day to see whether we're living our culture and what it means. Next, creating the team that helps shape the culture is paramount; we tell the story of how Aptiv's CEO built his team in chapter 3. We have to get alignment there to start moving. None of us can do this by ourselves. And then we all have to go out across the organization and communicate. I, and then other leaders, need to be able to crystallize our culture and share it in a way that has an impact on people and has meaning in their lives. We have to be out there talking about it as well as living it, all the time.

Doing all that might sound daunting at the best of times, and during an unprecedented period of uncertainty and volatility, such as the pandemic, it is harder but more important than ever. I am hopeful that this book will give leaders not only a sense of why culture matters in the long term, but also a sense of urgency to start now—and a straightforward framework to get started. Culture can seem vague and complicated, but this book will sharpen your understanding of how culture matters, why leaders need to focus on it, and how to link it to your strategy, leading to a set of specific questions to ask and steps to take.

I wish you all the best of luck as you shape your cultures to shape your futures.

Preface

When we set out to write this book, at the start of 2020, the topic of organizational culture was in the headlines and top of mind for leaders. Organizational culture was associated with enabling organizations to navigate myriad changes and disruption. In the context of challenges such as an increasingly digital world, a growing remote workforce, and the burgeoning importance of environmental, social, and governance strategy, organizations and their leaders needed to shape their cultures in order to shape their strategic futures.

Our intent in writing this book was to highlight culture's impact on engaging employees, delivering on strategy, and driving results, with case examples on how to shape culture. We wanted to tell stories about the many exemplary CEOs who have consciously shaped their organizations' cultures and to showcase how they unlocked the magic that enabled the success they experienced.

Well, we all know what happened in 2020: the unprecedented and most devastating disruption of our time, the global COVID-19 pandemic. People's experience of life dramatically shifted in a world suddenly rendered uncertain and unfamiliar. Faced with the biggest intractable problem in a generation, organizations dealt with disruption, discontinuity, and extreme challenges to their operating models. We had truly entered the realm of the "unknown unknown": an environment with problems which we did not understand and of which we were not even aware.

Leaders had to make major decisions quickly based upon limited or ambiguous information. Leadership demanded courage, a strong sense of purpose, and a capacity to demonstrate the confidence needed to engage and inspire a workforce filled with worry and uncertainty. Inclusive leadership and cultures of inclusion become the keys to unlocking thriving organizations. Words like "empathy" became very important; some leaders needed to fundamentally re-evaluate their personal style of leadership. Many CEOs found themselves leading their organizations while having no physical connection with their people, products, or customers.

At the time of publishing this book, the effects of the pandemic continue to affect us all as remote and hybrid workplaces have become the norm and leaders wrestle daily with "return to office" planning and scenarios. The world of work has been forever changed, and the collective pause around the globe has brought us back around to understanding that now, more than ever, culture matters. Malcolm Gladwell, author of *Blink* and *The Tipping Point*, put it well: "I've become more and more convinced...The company culture is the hardest thing to quantify, but the most important predictor of where a company is headed."

For us, the dramatic disruption of 2020 made us pause in our writing and consideration. Usefully, it also gave us time to gather more data, particularly about the ways that culture can positively impact the financial performance of organizations.

We talk more about the specific steps you can take in detail in chapter eight, but the overview is as follows: Heidrick & Struggles conducted a survey of 500 CEOs in nine different countries in early 2021; these organizations all had greater than $2.5 billion in annual revenue, and 39% earned over $10 billion.[1]

We discovered that there is a small group of CEOs embracing the focus on organizational culture, who we call the "culture accelerators" and who represented 11% of the CEOs surveyed. These culture accelerators had a clear focus on aligning culture with financial performance. Their companies demonstrate more than twice the compound annual growth rate (CAGR) for revenue over a three-year period compared to the 89% surveyed who were not as focused on aligning their culture with financial performance.

The year 2020 showed how fast the world can shift and change. As we continue to adapt to the "next normal," an intentional, sustained focus on culture has never been more important to enable a world better led. We hope this book will help you shape your culture and shape your future.

Chapter one

How culture makes a difference every day

At the height of the 2020 pandemic, Gail Boudreaux, Anthem, Inc., President and CEO, said, "Our Anthem culture and values serve as our foundation for giving back in our local communities. Our deeply committed associates have been giving back in various ways, such as online teaching outreach via phone or mail to those isolated at home, making masks for non-health care industry workers, and helping to provide personal care supplies and providing meal delivery to those homebound by the crisis across the country."[2] We worked with Boudreaux in her role as CEO at Anthem and, earlier, at United Healthcare. She is one of many CEOs at thousands of companies—including more than a third of the Fortune 500—with whom we have had the privilege of working with for more than 40 years.

Anthem, Inc., is a Fortune 500 health benefits service company that serves more than 107 million people. Boudreaux, who took the helm in 2018, believes strongly in organizational purpose and values as drivers of sustainability and results, and she focused on strengthening the company culture and emphasizing company values during her first year.

Anthem's stated purpose is "Improving Lives and Communities. Simplifying Healthcare. Expecting More." To support this, Anthem has upheld the values of leadership, community, integrity, agility, and diversity. That purpose and those values have served to inspire and engage more than 70,000 associates. Anthem has an active network of culture champions and internal facilitators who are carrying forward an insight-provoking culture experience and are driving engagement and accountability.

Anthem's adjusted net income showed an increase of 14.7% in 2020 over 2019, with an increase in quarterly dividend of nearly 19%.

Anthem's experience during one of the most tumultuous years in recent history underscores just how much cultural energy matters to the experience of employees and customers—and to driving bottom-line performance.

The compass for a future focus: Pointing toward purpose

Culture is not a program or an initiative—it's a drumbeat that runs through an organization. An authentically shared, socially meaningful purpose, like the one Boudreaux draws on, captures people's hearts and minds and becomes the core of authentic organizational culture.

Although this book is not about the changes that most of us saw and experienced throughout 2020, those events highlighted the terrifying speed with which the future can consume the present. They also highlighted the truth of the familiar saying that "culture eats strategy for breakfast." Leaders who had laid a solid culture foundation, authentically committed to a set of values, and defined and depended on an inspiring purpose helped their companies get through 2020 with more resilience and less turmoil. Those who hadn't often saw their organizations flounder.[3]

What makes the difference is that, when facing the same issues, organizations with thriving cultures deal with those issues more quickly and more effectively. Their leaders are more trusted. Their employees are more resilient and innovative. Their customers are more loyal. Their purpose-driven culture becomes the compass point that allows them to envision a clear future and thereby navigate through an unprecedented present. Such cultures allow leaders and organizations to be effectively future-focused, whatever challenges they are facing.

Socially meaningful organizational purpose has not always been at the core of thriving organizational cultures, but the role of such purpose has become ever more important over the 40 years we have been doing this work. The events of 2020 accelerated trends already in motion, notably the much-discussed shift from shareholder capitalism to stakeholder capitalism. In August 2019, the Business Roundtable, a community of 181 CEOs of leading global corporations, made headlines when it redefined the purpose of a corporation to promote "an economy that serves all Americans . . . [one that] allows each person to succeed through hard work and creativity and to lead a life of meaning and dignity."[4] From Tim Cook at Apple to Anders Gustafsson at Zebra Technologies, this group of CEOs publicly committed "to lead their companies for the benefit of all stakeholders—customers, employees, suppliers, communities, and shareholders."

In January 2020, Edelman released its annual Trust Barometer, which revealed "that despite a strong global economy and near full employment, none of the four societal institutions that the study measures—government, business, NGOs and media—*are as trusted*. The cause of this paradox can be found in people's fears about the future and their role in it. This is a wake-up call for our institutions to embrace a new way of effectively building trust: balancing competence with ethical behavior."[5]

Looking forward, as leaders seek to design and deliver on their strategies—whatever those strategies are and however quickly they change—clear and powerful purpose will help them create inspiration, alignment, and trust for all stakeholders. Shaping a thriving culture around that purpose will help leaders create meaningful, innovative, inclusive places of work that will attract and retain the best talent whatever changes come next, regardless of industry, where people are working, or whether those changes are planned or surprises.

How culture eats strategy

This example is a classic for a reason: Southwest Airlines. Southwest was one of the earliest companies to focus specifically on its culture and to be lauded consistently for the difference it has made in performance. Herb Kelleher, one of the founders, never believed that the discipline necessary to run an on-time airline with fantastic service was mutually exclusive with treating people like family and making work fun. He said, "A company is stronger if it is bound by love rather than by fear."[6] CEO Gary Kelly later expanded on this by saying, "We still believe that we are in the people business, and it's our people that make the culture so strong." Kelly said, "Our people serve our customers as if they were guests in their own home."[7] Today, customers feel the presence of Southwest's culture, whether they're connecting to a customer service rep, drawn in by the enthusiasm of the flight crew singing happy birthday to a surprised passenger, or listening to Gary Kelly speak to a group of employees about customer obsession. In a word, Southwest's culture is authentic, and people feel it. As a result of this commitment, Southwest has achieved 47 consecutive years of profitability.[8]

A memorable example of "culture eating strategy for breakfast" in this context is United Airlines. Seeing the success of Southwest, in 2003 United decided to pursue a similar low-cost, point-to-point strategy and launched TED, a new division. TED launched with all the fanfare you'd expect, even including a live concert with a popular star. The goal was to captivate customers on their maiden voyage. Toward that end, flight attendants had been trained to deliver a more light-hearted experience than the norm on United itself, and a look-alike fleet was assembled to capture two vacation markets.

However, after a mere six-year run, United shut TED down. Why? Missing from United's strategic venture was a culture that could actually deliver on the strategy. Where Southwest Airlines offered customers an experience rooted in its high-accountability, customer-focused, team-based, agile, quick-response culture, United's culture at the time was rules-centric, centralized in structure, and change-fatigued, causing resistance. Some years later, a former senior executive from TED, who was then at Boeing, told us that the company had reverse engineered pretty much everything about Southwest, even down to the ticketing. The one thing they had badly missed was that they simply did not have the leadership to bring Southwest's culture to life.

Such failure is the result of what we call "the jaws of culture." These jaws are a relatively invisible force in organizations that can make it really hard to get things done.

The jaws of culture

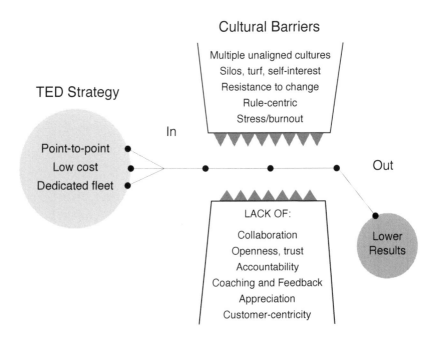

Cultural Barriers

Multiple unaligned cultures
Silos, turf, self-interest
Resistance to change
Rule-centric
Stress/burnout

TED Strategy

In

Point-to-point
Low cost
Dedicated fleet

Out

LACK OF:

Collaboration
Openness, trust
Accountability
Coaching and Feedback
Appreciation
Customer-centricity

Lower
Results

In other words, what Southwest did do, and TED did not, was ensure that its culture was fully aligned with its strategy. This alignment between culture and strategy—and the correlation with strong financial performance—was highlighted in our recent survey of CEOs around the world. CEOs who saw culture as an important driver of financial performance, thought it was important to align their cultures with their strategies, and made it a priority to work on culture. They succeeded more often in their culture-shaping goals and had higher revenue growth than other companies we surveyed.[9] We call these CEOs "culture accelerators," and we talk in more detail about them in chapter eight.

Strategy, structure, culture

ALIGNMENT

Purpose

Why We Exist
· Impact on the world

Strategy

Business Direction
· Strategy, vision, mission
· Value proposition
· Competitive advantage

Structure

Organization Capability
· Talent - competencies
· Organization design
· Systems and processes

Culture

Norms of Behaviors
· Collective habits
· Shared values
· Conditional beliefs

Our broader work shows that when that alignment is deep and real, it creates the rich, nourishing ground in which organizational culture thrives, specifically because of the link to strategic goals. In contrast, a lack of alignment is disruptive and a drain on the entire enterprise. With alignment, people are more likely to bring their discretionary energy to the enterprise, and their energy creates a learning mindset within a thriving culture. Think about the first time you went to a Disney theme park, or customized your coffee with a Starbucks barista, or stepped into an Apple store. Remember how instantly different it was? These brands have come to represent what an intentional, distinctly human, and very successful culture-driven experience can look like.

At the heart of any successful enterprise is the ability to execute better and faster than competitors. Culture is a primary enabler of execution, and, as such, it is the launchpad to success. Thinking about culture as a launchpad allows purpose and values to be positioned in an effective manner.

Culture launching pad

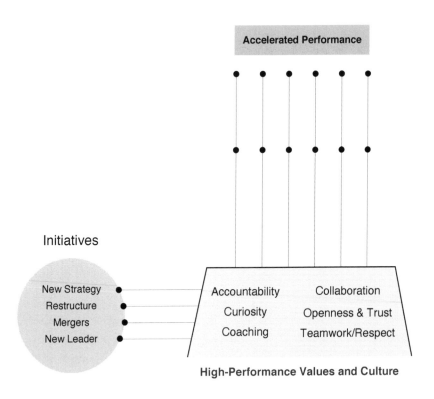

©2021 Heidrick & Struggles International Inc., All rights reserved.

Culture and transformation

Thriving cultures that are aligned with strategy are also central to helping companies navigate planned change toward a better future. Common situations include mergers and acquisitions, digital transformations, and improved diversity, equity, and inclusion initiatives. But any major transformation process—from immediate crisis response to long-planned strategic shifts—requires a supportive culture to be successful.

Francesco Starace, the CEO of Enel, the Italy-based power company, for example, views culture as key to successful digital transformation. The digitization of electricity grids and a shift toward a platform-based model for electricity delivery are at the core of Enel's strategic vision. Starace believes that there is no such thing as a digital culture—there are simply powerful cultures that will accelerate digital transformation. At a November 2020 Fortune CEO Roundtable, the discussion turned to the point that digital transformation has to be led by the CEO because of its strategic importance, but CEOs often lack the knowledge to make critical technology decisions. Starace offered the recommendation to "create a risk-taking culture."[10] Noting that utilities are inherently risk-averse, he sponsored an employee contest on the topic of "My Greatest Failure," which helped to shift leader and employee mindsets and behaviors at Enel and to build comfort with greater risk in order to support the digital transformation.

Similarly, there are many examples of M&A deals that are trumpeted with great fanfare, only to quietly fade away into disappointment and failure. The desired outcomes are not reached, morale drops, and key people head for the door. According to years of research collected in a recent *Harvard Business Review* report, the failure rate for M&A is between 70% and 90%.[11] At the top of the list of reasons for failure sits culture, including both clashing cultures and traits that inhibit successful integration. Indeed, all the best revenue modeling, synergy planning, resource allocation, and other myriad practical and financial details fade away in the face of legacy cultures.

On the other hand, in 2000, when GlaxoSmithKline was formed by the merger of Glaxo Wellcome and SmithKline Beecham, leaders recognized that they were dealing with multiple cultures from fourteen different legacy organizations. They needed to create a single global culture and set of values so people felt led in a consistent manner, no matter where they were in the world. GSK experienced the payoff for having enterprise-wide engagement, having teams that formed much more quickly under a common platform and leaders who are far more connected because they use a common language underpinned by common values.

Other examples of companies that have invested in broad transformations that succeeded because they were grounded in great purpose and values, with leadership teams and boards that were aligned behind that purpose, include the following:

- **Citibank**, which recognized that many financial service organizations have become commoditized data businesses and that a unified culture would have the largest positive effect on the customer experience. The organization called this the "Power of One," and it became an underlying narrative for their new strategy.

- **Proximus**, a Belgian telecommunications company, which knew that its strategy of customer retention through integrating fixed, mobile, entertainment, and broadband businesses would fail unless it could eliminate the silos that separated people and information. Its "Good to Gold" culture has enabled customer retention and promoted significant growth.

- **Rolls-Royce**, which had a legacy of engineering excellence in making gas turbine engines but came to understand that its long-term revenue would come from service relationships. Its leaders shaped a customer-focused culture, called "High Performance Culture," and made it as important as the engineering mindset, threading it through every aspect of the business.

- **Thomson Reuters**, which moved from using 25 different technology platforms around the world to a single, integrated global platform because its leaders recognized they had to promote a "One Company" attitude and mindset to succeed.

These examples share a common approach: a commitment to communicating future-focused culture imperatives to everyone, everywhere, through deliberate words and actions, with purpose and conviction.

Focusing on your future

Intentionally developing your culture, linking purpose and strategy, and institutionalizing shared values, behaviors, and norms, as the CEOs described in this chapter and so many peers have done, serves as a powerful launchpad for alignment and acceleration. Leaders who shape culture this way continually articulate and activate deliberate actions to maintain alignment of the culture with growth strategy. They are purposeful, intentional, and open to personal change, and they empower everyone in the process to be unafraid of what the future might hold. Employees have a voice and are actively engaged in living the organization's values. These organizations are purpose-driven and characterized by vitality and a growth mindset. They greet disruptions by carrying forward the strengths of their culture's legacy, ready to pivot and evolve their legacy culture to shape the future. They lean into the future.

There is no one-size-fits-all approach when it comes to culture-shaping. That's a good thing. People are not one-size-fits-all beings. However, there are common elements to thriving, adaptive, powerful cultures, and there are four foundational principles that serve as keys to shaping and maintaining them: purposeful leadership, personal change, broad engagement, and systemic alignment.

In the rest of this book, we will explore in more detail those characteristics and principles, as well as metrics to track progress and our best insights into shaping and maintaining culture in a hybrid work environment. We will share practical information you need to succeed. Our goal is simple: to empower you with the mindsets, case studies, research, and resources you need to intentionally and continuously shape your culture and your future.

Key takeaways

- Future-focused cultures start with purposeful, future-focused leaders.

- Strategy, structure, culture alignment, and a people-first focus are key to the successful transformation of your company's culture.

- Culture must be intentionally shaped in order to accelerate future performance.

- Foundational principles and culture-change strategies must work in tandem for driving thriving, high-performing organizations.

Reflections

- What is your organization's culture today? How does it feel?

- How does your organization define culture?

- What disruptions and challenges are your organization facing today?

- Think about whether your organization's culture is ready to meet and adapt to the *future*. Where are your strengths? What gaps need to be addressed to secure *future* success?

- How has your organization's culture aided or hindered your employees' resilience through the pandemic? What have you learned that you want to integrate into a future-focused culture?

Chapter two

The principles of creating a healthy cultural ecosystem

We like to say that we're a family, and in turn, we want to treat our Customers as if they were guests in our own home. And the nice thing about Southwest, it's just in our DNA—that's who we are.[12]

—Gary Kelly, CEO, Southwest Airlines

As we noted, Southwest is a classic example of culture's link to financial success, and it is worth exploring in a bit more depth because culture was at the core from the company's founding. In 1967, in a hotel bar in San Antonio, Herb Kelleher[13] and Rollin King[14] drew the first three routes for a hypothetical airline on the back of a cocktail napkin: three lines connecting Dallas, Houston, and San Antonio. In the drawing, they outlined their idea for something they wanted, something that didn't exist—yet. The central organizing idea that still lies at the core of the company was one of simplicity: point-to-point-service, use of the same aircraft across the whole fleet, on-time departures and arrivals, and no frills. But the key component required to truly set them apart from the industry was a positive, energetic, and customer-focused culture that has made Southwest the envy of its rivals for many years.

Culture is an organization's living, breathing, evolving habits, mindsets, behaviors, and values—the glue holding organizations together. It's an ecosystem. Like any ecosystem, if it's healthy, like a clean stream, forest, or garden, it teems with life and promotes new growth. If any aspect of the ecosystem is unhealthy or toxic, it diminishes the life force of everything in it. Culture sets the living context for everything else in the organization.

Everything? Yes, everything: brand, recruiting and retention, service, supply chain, information security, new product development, revenue, and reputation, to name just a few. Culture either attracts people, ideas, and energy, or it stifles and repels them. Unfortunately, there's not much middle ground.

Many leaders begin a culture journey by identifying the toxic things, the things holding them back, and then seek to change or improve those influences, thinking, "We need to be better at collaboration, create more accountability, and focus more intently on the customer," for example. This isn't wrong: toxic cultures, which may have formed by default, can lead to significant operational risks, such as people hiding failures out of fear, creating false or misleading records to support performance claims, or not bringing up new opportunities because senior leaders don't listen.

However, while these considerations are important, many leaders miss out on the need to create a compelling and inspirational narrative connecting culture directly to the purpose of the business and how it will fulfill that purpose to meet strategic goals: the positive story.

So, which aspects of culture contribute most to ecosystem health, and what are the four principles of moving from toxic to healthy?

A healthy cultural ecosystem

A recent study of companies we've worked with,[15] both financially higher- and lower-performing, found that leaders at the high performers demonstrate seven characteristics we call the "flourishing factors." Almost all of these flourishing factors focus on the relationships *among* team members rather than on individual experiences.

- There is two-way, frequent, and open communication.

- There is great openness to change.

- There is a high level of customer-service consciousness and customer focus.

- Teamwork and mutual support and cooperation is the norm.

- People are flexible.

- There is a high level of openness and trust among people.

- There is an environment that is optimistic and forgiving.

These factors underlie foundational cultural drivers we have identified, grounded in decades of research and work with hundreds of organizations that were focused on building high-performance, thriving cultures and were led by CEOs who were intentional and purposeful about transforming those cultures. With the flourishing factors at the root, the organizational and relationship drivers that serve as the engine for high performance are the following:

The essential dimensions

- **Collaboration and trust:** Creating frequent two-way communication, openness, and trust among people, with high levels of feedback and coaching.

- **Appreciation and recognition:** Appreciating and valuing people; recognizing and rewarding performance.

- **Positive spirit and vitality:** Creating an environment where there is teamwork, mutual support, and cooperation between and among people and where people are fun to be around, proud of what they do, and willing to put in effort beyond normal expectations.

- **Agility, innovation, and growth:** Encouraging people to innovate, create, and be open to change; empowering people and having a bias toward action and an urgency to move forward.

- **Direction and purpose:** Providing a sense of direction and purpose; having a clear alignment connection to achieving the organization's strategic goals.

- **Ethics and integrity:** Acting with honesty and integrity; treating core values and ethics as very important; making decisions for the greater good of the organization; seeing healthy differences and diversity as strengths.

- **Performance orientation:** Having high expectations for performance and accountability for actions and results; being a self-starter.

- **Customer and quality focus:** Having a high focus on and awareness of quality and customer service.

These cultural drivers align with the capabilities that, as other work at our firm has shown, accelerate performance at the leader, team, and organizational levels. We will discuss this more in later chapters and in the appendix.

From here to the aspirational there

Leaders can, and should, undertake surveys of employees and use focus groups and broader discussions to understand how much—or how little—their current culture includes these elements. (See chapter seven for more detail on metrics.)

Knowing which aspects of culture most promote health and where those factors stand today, leaders can employ four fundamental principles to shape thriving, high-performing culture. These are based on our four decades of work; we show how CEOs have put each one into play in chapters three through six.

Four principles

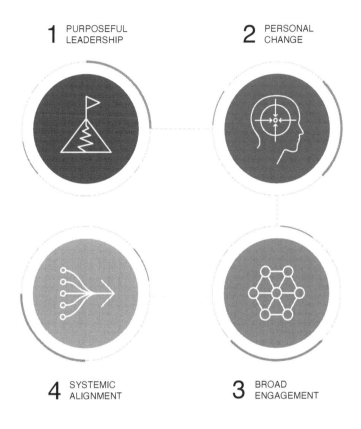

1 PURPOSEFUL
LEADERSHIP

2 PERSONAL
CHANGE

4 SYSTEMIC
ALIGNMENT

3 BROAD
ENGAGEMENT

Principle 1: Thriving cultures require *purposeful leadership*.
Purpose-driven leaders who are intentionally committed to
the organization and its culture cast a long shadow of positive
influence. In his dissertation, *The Personality of Organizations*,
Dr. Larry Senn espoused that organizations are shadows of
their leaders. He understood that the shadow the senior team
casts can have both good and bad impacts. According to Senn,
when it comes to the shadows leaders cast, two key questions
to regularly ask inside your organization are, "What's the good

news?" and, "What's the bad news?" Purposeful leaders also uphold organizational purpose that serves as a culture compass, engaging and inspiring employees towards personal meaning and connection.

Principle 2: Transformation is rooted in *personal change*. This principle challenges leaders to model openness to personal change. You've got to be uncomfortable at times in order to be able to say, "I need to change, or we need to change, in order to do the right thing here." If culture is the collective thinking in an organization, the importance of the perspective and health of leaders is key.

Leaders need to be able to take a hard look in the mirror so they can make an authentic commitment to humility and to doing the right thing. We have all seen and experienced what happens to the credibility of a decision when a leader says one thing and does something completely different.

Principle 3: *Broad engagement* is key for the culture to be lived. This means culture permeates every corner, office, and person across the organization. From the board and top team to the frontline employees, including temporary or contract staff, the culture must live inside of everyone. There has to be broad engagement in order to inspire and support all employees, especially those on the front line, with the tools to make good decisions every day for customers.

The behavior of the front line, either in support of the culture and values or in defiance and chipping away at them, will define the customer's experience. Broad engagement of the culture is at the root of the employee value proposition, which in turn makes or breaks the customer value proposition.

Principle 4: Thriving into the future requires *systemic alignment*. The culture and values have to be not only integrated into the minds and hearts of all employees, but also "hardwired" into all of the systems of the organization. From communications and HR systems and processes to operations, marketing, finance, and every other function, culture must be congruent at every level and in every policy. This is a leadership, systemic, and organizational design challenge.

Shaping a culture is a challenging undertaking under any circumstance. What we know is that while CEOs may understand or recognize company culture, many are not confident about how to shape it into something powerful and focused that drives performance. As a result, they take different tacks. They delegate the responsibility or allow cultural initiatives to stop and start. In some cases, they take the "if it ain't broke, don't fix it" approach.

Many well-intentioned efforts achieve only superficial changes that cannot be sustained. This is often due to a narrow or incomplete vision of the existing culture, a lack of data, or a lack of a plan to align it with the company's strategy and vision. By starting with a clear view of the existing company culture, senior leaders can better articulate how their organization's culture will directly impact the performance of the business. They can then identify and prioritize immediate areas of focus and continue to shape the culture to achieve the desired impact.

Key takeaways

- Culture is a living ecosystem that must be nurtured and intentionally developed to ensure positive impact.

- Failure to intentionally shape culture opens the door to risk. Purposeful, future-focused cultures secure mindsets and behaviors that deliver performance and minimize risk.

- Culture must be systemically "hardwired" into the fabric of the organization's HR systems, quality and operational excellence initiatives, and employee and customer experience to be sustainable.

Reflections

- How are you nurturing and continuing to develop your organization's cultural ecosystem?

- What are the critical mindsets and behaviors required to future-proof your organization and deliver on your strategic ambition?

- Which "hardwired" elements are strengths in your organization? Which represent gaps?

Chapter three

Purposeful leadership

Kevin Clark, the CEO of Aptiv, an industrial technology company, says he was able to lead the organization along a path from its roots as an automotive supplier to its current reputation as one of the world's top sustainable and innovative companies in the industrial tech sector because:

> Aptiv has a diverse, complex organization and DNA. Its successful transformation from a legacy automotive supplier to becoming a leading industrial tech company is predicated upon living our core values and enabling our purpose to make the world safer, greener, and more connected. The future of Aptiv and the future of mobility rest in making our culture real every day. Aptiv's culture starts with me—and with each one of our employees.

But Aptiv didn't stop there. In 2019, the company embarked on a multiyear, enterprise-wide cultural transformation initiative focused on mobilizing, aligning, adapting, and energizing their worldwide workforce in support of its next strategic transformation. Launching a series of surveys, evaluating cultural strengths, and identifying areas of opportunity, Aptiv focused on the key cultural factors proven to drive operational performance and employee engagement.

With purpose and passion, Clark personally led the development of a set of organizational values grounded in the mantra, "We do the right thing the right way." These values and guiding behaviors, along with the company's mission to "enable a safer, greener, and more connected future of mobility," have become the compass point for the organization.

Clark launched the "Mobilizing Our Culture" journey with conviction and commitment by sharing with his organization his personal experiences and how he personally related to the values, and by engaging his leadership team in similarly taking ownership of the culture from a personal perspective. Attending six sessions around the globe, he invited his top 450 leaders to join him in making the values real at Aptiv. The journey continues as Aptiv has rolled out workshops globally, building a critical mass of commitment with over 4,000 leaders. Each session is focused on leading through culture by embodying values and behaviors in order to fulfill Aptiv's purpose and execute its strategy.

Honing organizational purpose

Clark was able to achieve so much in part because Aptiv established a clear, inspiring organizational purpose. As human beings, we have a deep and innate need for meaning and purpose in our lives—a need that, for many people, has only deepened since the beginning of 2020. Most of us feel the need to be a part of something that has depth, emotional commitment, and a sense of belonging. A socially valuable organizational purpose can be the central organizing thought at the core of every element of a business. It should inform decisions, be at the core of the integrity of an organization, and guide long-term strategy while overcoming short-term issues and market challenges. Having such a purpose is ever more crucial post-2020, as we discussed in chapter one. It is a challenge leaders must meet in order to engage employees and consumers with their organization's purpose, mission, and values.

Furthermore, it is currently well understood that an organization with a clear purpose is much more powerful in the marketplace. Data from our Organization Acceleration Questionnaire (see appendix) highlights the power of purpose. Any organization is more competitive and more profitable if it is clear about why it exists beyond simply making profit. The rise in purpose-driven advocacy is a challenge for leaders to either engage employees and consumers on issues that are aligned with their organization's purpose, mission, and values—or fail.

Clarity of purpose

The impact of clarity of purpose on organizational acceleration drivers

■ High-purpose organizations ■ Low-purpose organizations

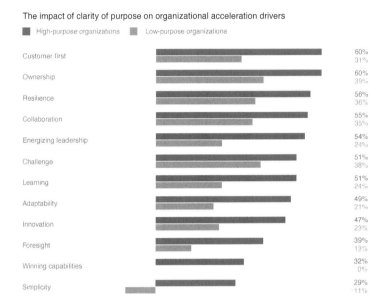

Customer first	60% / 31%
Ownership	60% / 39%
Resilience	56% / 36%
Collaboration	55% / 35%
Energizing leadership	54% / 24%
Challenge	51% / 38%
Learning	51% / 24%
Adaptability	49% / 21%
Innovation	47% / 23%
Foresight	39% / 13%
Winning capabilities	32% / 0%
Simplicity	29% / 11%

Source: Analysis of Heidrick & Struggles proprietary data covering 45,000 people at 41 organizations

Some organizations, like Aptiv, have a clear and well-understood purpose. For organizations that don't, defining such a purpose successfully must begin with intentional commitment by the CEO and executive team. That is because the development of such a purpose can directly challenge a number of assumptions about how the company is run, what it stands for, the customers it desires to serve, and the way it goes to market. These are often difficult and far-reaching decisions. Having the tenacity to see them through will align the executive team around a common purpose. It will also sharpen the strategic intent of the business and secure a strong sense of ownership by the CEO and executive team.

Our study of purpose-driven organizations has led us to recommend two steps in developing and activating organizational purpose.[16]

Step 1: Discover and articulate

To follow the tenets of a purpose-driven culture, take a three-pronged approach:

- Look from the outside in: what does your brand mean to customers? What is your employee promise? Align the answers to these questions with the articulation of your purpose.

- Look from the inside out: what do leaders authentically believe? The purpose statement should reflect core values and be actionable. The shadow of the leader should be in harmony with the spirit of the statement.

- Look from a capability standpoint: what is your organization really good at? What core capability can you leverage, what makes you money, and what makes people passionate about you?

Acknowledge that the purpose statement is not static; it is a living and breathing organism that will need to evolve and adjust along with company strategy.

Step 2: Provide clarity for decision-making and align the purpose with values and leadership behaviors

A clear, compelling purpose statement is a litmus test for decision-making and actions, serving as a source of checks and balances. In this regard, communication and reinforcement of purpose is important.

When a company can crisply define its purpose, our research has shown, employees rate their organizations higher across all acceleration factors in our META model than those in low-purpose organizations. META is the ability to mobilize, execute and transform with agility. (See appendix for more on tools to measure META.)

Delta CEO Ed Bastian provided a clear example of alignment between purpose and behaviors in an e-mail to all employees early in the pandemic: "Your veteran colleagues will tell you that we have been through turbulent times before, and what has always carried us through has been our commitment to our values, our culture, and each other. I am confident that we will emerge from this crisis as a strong, trusted global brand that truly connects the world like no other. And we will be stronger for having gone through this experience."[17]

The message rang true for employees because Bastian's actions were aligned with his words. He made sensible fiscal decisions to stabilize the company's balance sheet, for example, including committing to forgo 100% of his salary.

This example highlights something we have seen over and over in organizations of all kinds and sizes: relying on an organization's values is possible only when those values are real and modeled by leaders at all levels of the organization.

CVS: A bold yet profitable leap toward purpose

CVS Caremark was formed in the U.S. in 2007 as a combination of CVS, a retail chain of drugstores, and Caremark, a distribution company for pharmaceutical products for drug stores, hospitals, and healthcare institutions. The leaders of the new business wanted to move away from retail and to be thought of as being in the healthcare business. A part of their transformation was to create a single, clear purpose statement. The CEO and executive team spent time off-site with our team and, as a part of their alignment process, defined the new purpose of CVS Caremark: helping people on their path to better health.

One aspect of the company's current business that was at odds with this statement was the fact that, prior to 2014, CVS Caremark generated $2 billion in annual revenue from the sale of cigarettes.[18] So, in a courageous decision, the leaders decided that a company committing to this new purpose could not justify selling cigarettes. In the face of huge pressure from investors, they stopped. Everyone waited for the inevitable financial fallout—but it didn't happen.

CVS lost the $2 billion in front-of-house revenue but gained the respect of millennials, along with a significant uptick in overall revenue. It also became a talent magnet for people who wanted to work at a company that stood for something important. Within 12 months, CVS had posted an increase of almost 10% in revenue, operating profit up by 4% and a stock price up by 66%. It turned out to be a smart move, one that was driven by purposeful leadership in service of a socially meaningful purpose.

Start with personal commitment and a link to the organizational purpose

Any leader who is serious about shaping culture by design, and not by default, has to be all-in: completely, purposefully committed. For leaders, being all-in equates to 24/7 purposeful leadership, where every action taken demonstrates intention. When leaders energize their companies, our research shows, employees rate the companies' performance to be twice as strong as others.

Purposeful leadership has two dimensions.

The first is an intentional commitment to the culture. It's a mindset fueled by a recognition of the power, importance, and impact of culture, as well as the importance of putting people first. It's authentic. You simply can't put culture first without putting people first. Great leaders recognize that culture both drives performance and unleashes the humanity of the organization in the process. Those leaders are intentional in the way they reflect that connection.

A leader's mindset is often more visible, more keenly felt, and more closely scrutinized than most leaders realize. We draw this perspective from our research[19] on how an organization's culture is deeply influenced by the "shadow of the leader," a wide scope of influence that transmits the leader's intent and commitment throughout the organization.[20] We'll go more deeply into this research in the next section. Suffice it to say, the leader's shadow is profound and supports the momentum of a vibrant culture. Or, in particularly notable and painful cases, it does not.

The second dimension is connecting to organizational purpose as the foundation for purposeful leadership. As leaders become purposeful and intentional about their cultures, they become

- By building great teams that are aligned to the purpose and have an almost innate understanding of what they're doing and why they're doing it

The U.S. National Basketball Association players: Supporting fundamental social change

Following the shooting of Jacob Blake in Kenosha, Wisconsin, in the summer of 2020, the state's NBA team, the Milwaukee Bucks, went on strike immediately, sitting out the 2020 NBA finals, visibly and vocally protesting in support of the Black Lives Matter movement that had taken on unprecedented power after the murder of George Floyd that May. LeBron James, one of the league's biggest stars, and the rest of the teams followed suit, sitting out the next playoff games, withholding their value as athletes until they could voice their concerns directly to their team owners.

They negotiated an agreement with franchise owners to address social causes,[23] making voter registration a focus. As a result of their strike, at least 20 NBA arenas became polling sites for the U.S. presidential election. The NBA players used their platforms and their voices to inspire change with an unprecedented get-out-the vote effort. They stayed true to their purpose. Modelling their message personally, they moved their own NBA league voter registration from 22% in 2016 to 96% in 2020. Twenty teams are at 100% registration.

Exemplifying how to truly embrace purpose, James said, "If we want change, we need to make it ourselves."[24]

Key takeaways

The core components of purposeful leadership are the following:

- Purposeful, intentional commitment to culture is key to transformation. The leader's commitment to culture casts a shadow that has the potential to quickly inspire engagement, alignment, and performance or to undermine culture efforts.

- A commitment to purpose positively influences business results. When aligned with strategy, purpose has the potential to elevate that strategy and to deliver on its promise to customers. Purpose impacts performance through energizing leadership.

- Purposeful leaders drive greater clarity in their organization, which leads to increased speed of decision-making and ease of execution.

Reflections

- What is your organization's purpose? Is it well understood, embraced, and lived throughout the organization? If so, how is it impacting leadership behavior? How is it impacting results?

- How have you demonstrated purposeful leadership in your organization? What more can you do to demonstrate intentional commitment to culture?

- How has your purpose enabled you to navigate through a crisis or inspired an enduring culture in challenging times like the pandemic?

- Looking to the *future*, how will your purpose help your company reach its ambition?

Chapter four

Personal change— developing and sustaining growth mindsets

In a speech at Florida's Palm Beach Atlantic University, David Novak, retired CEO and chairman of Yum! Brands, the U.S. fast-food holding company, said the following:

> I believe that leadership is a privilege. I also believe that all people have an inherent desire to make a positive difference through the work that they do. If you can establish an environment where every person feels that they have a chance to contribute, you've created a situation where people can do great things.[25]

As we have worked with Novak over the years, we learned that his belief that leadership is a privilege was evident in his humility and passion for unleashing people's potential. His understanding of the impact of personal change was evident in how he lived a growth mindset in his own leadership journey and in how he challenged other leaders to personally commit through the importance he placed on culture: "Leaders cast a long shadow." Because they do so, they must consistently "use the awesome power of recognition," especially if they hope to attract and retain committed, loyal talent to their organizations.

Among the ways Novak fostered a recognition and appreciation culture were special awards he created to acknowledge employees and culture champions. Among these treasured awards were iconic items, such as rubber chickens (yes, really—they were a highly prized award!), plastic "cheese heads," and Taco Bell sauce packets accompanied by a personal statement of recognition and a monetary gift. Our experience has always been that Novak lives life and leadership in gratitude. This powerful shadow has contributed to the culture legacy he "heartwired and hardwired" into the Yum! organization.

From habits to "aha!"

To understand the dynamics of culture, leaders need to understand human beings. We are pattern-making creatures. We get through life by creating habits and establishing well-understood routines. These habits and routines are the norms that lie at the heart of any organization's culture.

Habits and routines are far more than just mental and emotional processes. They are rooted in our biology. New tasks, habits, motor skills, and relationships create new neural pathways in our brains, so changing habits really do become hardwired into our neural systems.[26] This is good news and bad news. The good news is that these habits allow us to function in an ever more complex world and can help groups of people navigate complex systems across the enterprise. The bad news is that, in times of constant change, what used to be the right way of doing something will no longer achieve the desired result. Purpose-driven leaders are more challenged than ever to learn themselves, and help their organizations learn, how to develop new mindsets and behaviors in support of their purpose and strategy—and to ensure those mindsets can continue to evolve as the organization does.

Adults learn best from practical, goal-oriented, and respectful environments. But most of all, adults learn and grow through experience. One of the most powerful ways we learn is with insight gained through reflection. Ruth Helyer, a thought leader in adult learning, conducted research on work-based learning. She noted, "People consciously reflect in order to understand events in their lives and as a consequence hopefully add and enhance meaning."[27]

It is the insightful "aha" moment that rewires the neural network and shifts our perspective. For leaders, this can be a powerful moment that can be harnessed for personal change.

Furthermore, in our work with organizations, we have seen that with enough shifts in individual perspectives, cultures can shift, too. From the leader's perspective, individual insights are generative engines for shaping culture. The most powerful and productive cultures occur where the leader shapes the climate for individual and team insight, reflection, and action. The cumulative impact allows leaders to shift organizational values and behaviors both intellectually and emotionally. This is the foundation of sustainable culture.

Insight is now commonly recognized as a fundamental driver of leadership, training, innovation, and forward momentum generally in organizational cultures. Practices that generate insights need to be cultivated and reinforced in everyday environments to stick. This is where most traditional corporate learning programs fade. An array of diverse practices can be used to generate and sustain learning from insight. Among them, "engineered epiphanies," described in the afterword by Dr. Larry Senn, effectively unfreeze habits and behaviors to enable insights and actions.

From insights to personal change

Creating change takes more than tools and opportunities, of course. Leaders who really lean into authentically living their intentions with an openness and a willingness to embrace personal change, who live the difference between intellectually committing and being all-in, are those who can motivate their teams and organizations to change as well.

The intersection between individual purpose and values and those of the organization is at the very heart of an organization's ability to foster engagement and commitment. The bridge at this intersection is framed by an employee's sense of belonging, willingness to be open and trusting, and a sense of feeling empowered to act.

In understanding why we do what we do, it's always worth looking at the two primary modes of motivation: extrinsic and intrinsic. Each can have different effects on people's behaviors and how they pursue their goals and activities.

- Extrinsic motivation is when you do something or behave in a way that gets a reward or avoids punishment, not because it is necessarily enjoyable.

- Intrinsic motivation is when you do something because you love it or find it interesting.

It is the blend of these two that can create a sense of self-determination in people that is at the heart of accountability. That blending will draw on reflection and insight.

The Industrial Age "carrot-and-stick" approach developed by Jeremy Bentham, an English philosopher known as the founder of modern utilitarianism, was based on the premise that desired behavior would be rewarded with financial and non-financial benefits, while punitive actions would be taken to push an individual toward desired behavior. More than two centuries later, while there is no dispute that behaviors are required to generate results, the underlying drivers of behavior still often go undervalued.

Indeed, as many organizations have discovered over the years, defining a clear set of behaviors and announcing them to great fanfare does not mean that people will behave that way. We have all had the experience of getting the "We are One Team" T-shirt. The initiative launches to improve teamwork, the posters go up on the walls, the screen savers show up on laptops, and yet little changes over time.

The results cone

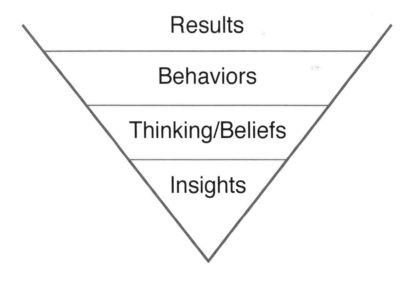

The "Results Cone" is a simple yet powerful model of how insight shifts behavior. Consider the top of the cone, the word "results." In organizations, the messages employees hear most frequently are about the importance of generating results. And most, if not all, employees have a desire to succeed in delivering results, not only for extrinsic reasons like pay increases and promotions, but also, at purpose-driven organizations, for intrinsic ones like contributing to a meaningful purpose. People's behaviors and actions day in and day out are at the core of generating results, both personally and organizationally.

What drives our behaviors? Our beliefs do. These are patterns of thinking influenced by a myriad of factors, including culture, familial roots, experiences, and biases that are unconscious and beneath the surface. We have a never-ending stream of thought that provides the narrative for our experience of life. It is the one voice that we truly listen to. It guides us in all the decisions that we make and is an innate force that mostly serves us well, but it can also be very unreliable. This internal dialogue is the summation of our beliefs, our life's experience, and our hopes and fears. In *Hamlet*, Shakespeare writes, "There is nothing either good or bad, but thinking makes it so." Sustained thought-habits and beliefs drive the behaviors that make or break our results. The only reliable means of shaking our beliefs and shifting our mindsets is insight.

To examine the impact of a belief on results, let's take an example where a leader carries this underlying belief: "If you want the job done right, do it yourself." It may have been a mantra the leader heard in her upbringing or in her career progression. This belief may be influenced by a controlling style of leadership. At the core, however, it may drive that leader to hold the cards, micromanage, and thus fail to delegate appropriately. Heroic behavior may take over, and the leader may believe she is doing great work.

Those behaviors may deliver short-term results, but they will also invariably result in a sense of overload and unmotivated direct reports who ultimately give up trying to contribute. At some point, results will suffer, and that leader will be left believing the poor results were caused by employees who didn't carry their share of the workload. Until a leader has an insight that motivates her to change the belief driving the behavior, results won't change.

If the leader gains significant insight through, for example, a supervisor's or direct report's feedback about how her beliefs are failing to deliver sustainable results, she may have the moment of clarity that she needs to start to trust team members, delegate more, and control less.

For leaders to be most effective, they need to coach and guide at the level of each team member's thinking. The "why" beneath behavior is as important as the behavior itself and is the only way to understand what will motivate change. The role of leaders is to provide opportunities for insight, for shifts in belief, and ultimately for sustainable shifts in behavior.

For leaders to shape a culture successfully, effectively, and for the long term, they must be open to personal change and insight. Their personal change will accelerate organizational change.

The impact of the shadow of the leader

All this means that the capacity of leadership teams (and all teams) for personal change is a predictor of success or failure when trying to shape culture. We all know leaders who have fatally undermined a transformation process by saying one thing and doing something else. A simple example is when a senior leader passionately states that collaboration across the organization is vital to success, and then they do something that is in their naked self-interest.

The shadow of the leader can also have influence in very subtle ways. Sometimes doing nothing is a very powerful statement, whether for good or for bad. What a leader permits, they also promote. For example, if a leader sees or is aware of discriminatory activity and does nothing about it, then what they are really saying is that they don't mind if people behave that way.

On the other hand, the most difficult moment—and most powerful opportunity for any organization—is when a leader who drives strong business results but who does not live the company values is held accountable for behavior or even let go. That action sends the most visible message possible to employees that culture matters and that living the values is table stakes for every leader, without exception.

Simple or complex, the shadow of the leader is a powerful phenomenon, one that must never be underestimated by the leader or the organization around them.

In the context of culture-shaping, leaders need to show their organizations that they care about the change they are asking others to embrace. The simplest way to do this is to model that change, as we discussed in chapter three.

Creating the context for insight: From fixed to growth mindsets via psychological safety

To get to the insights that can shift beliefs and therefore behaviors, people need to be open to change. That means breaking the power of habit: unfreezing current habits, mindsets, and behaviors to make way for new thinking, new possibilities, and new behaviors.

As adults, many of us have lost sight of our potential for fresh thinking because our habits have been long-lasting and have often served us well. In our experience, however, the pattern of unfreezing—awareness—is key to personal change. A willingness and a persistent commitment to improve over time is known as a growth mindset. Personal change and a growth mindset are critical companions to fostering agility, innovation, and continuous learning and development.

In *Mindset: The New Psychology of Success*, Carol Dweck, an American psychologist and author, writes, "What are the consequences of thinking that your intelligence or personality is something you can develop, as opposed to something that is a fixed, deep-seated trait?"[28] Dweck first became interested in this topic by observing that it was not always the brightest kids who did well in tests and puzzles. When given a test that was slightly too hard for them, a group of 10-year-olds behaved in very different ways. Some expressed disappointment that the test was too difficult and felt that they had failed by not getting top marks and that their intellect had been found wanting in the face of a challenge. Others expressed delight at the challenge, knowing that they would learn and become better as a result of the effort they were putting in. Dweck saw this as a core example of two different mindsets people may have: fixed mindsets and growth mindsets. Which one a person has makes a significant difference in their lives and the success they achieve.

The fixed mindset about talent and learning shows up in a belief that a person's qualities, personality, and intelligence are static and unchanging. People with this mindset believe that success is dependent on using that fixed, permanent, unchanging capability to create successful outcomes.

The growth mindset seeks challenges and believes experience is a springboard for growth and stretching abilities. People with this mindset believe intelligence and talents can be developed, and they look for these qualities. They believe that effort is the path to mastery and that mistakes are an essential part of learning on that path. In other words, they see failure as an opportunity to learn. A growth mindset embraces challenges and sees possibilities. It's easy to see why leaders need a growth mindset and need to encourage everyone in their organizations to have one, too.

People with a growth mindset have a passion for learning and improving their capabilities. They embrace challenges and persist in the face of setbacks. They thrive on challenges and are often highly successful when times are at their most demanding because they believe they can find a way that may not be immediately apparent.

It's not that fixed-mindset leaders can't be successful in challenging times. But people with a fixed mindset may not access all the intellectual and emotional capabilities available to them. We know that as people feel more pressured and frustrated at a lack of progress, those with a fixed mindset may lose access to their emotional quotient (EQ). That loss of EQ means that people also lose their perspective, get irritated by others, and consequently lose the ability to engage their teams and inspire their best performance.

Self-awareness of the impact of our moods and emotional state is foundational to unlocking a leader's access to greater EQ and a growth mindset. Indeed, maintaining a growth mindset requires slowing down, listening deeply, paying attention, observing your own experience, and tuning into another person's experience.

The "Mood Elevator" concept, developed by Dr. Larry Senn,[29] can be a powerful tool to foster insight into whether you are in a growth mindset or a fixed mindset.

The mood elevator

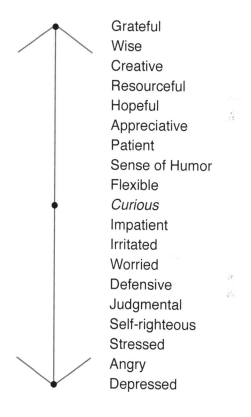

Grateful
Wise
Creative
Resourceful
Hopeful
Appreciative
Patient
Sense of Humor
Flexible
Curious
Impatient
Irritated
Worried
Defensive
Judgmental
Self-righteous
Stressed
Angry
Depressed

At the top of the Mood Elevator are emotional states associated with operating at our best, with gratitude at the top.

Remember David Novak's experience of leadership as a privilege? Neuroscience research sheds a light on why. David Rock, the founder of the NeuroLeadership Institute, focuses on the importance of creating psychological safety: "The brain classifies everything into either danger or opportunity, but it's a continuum, not a binary." Therefore, "managing [one's] 'threat state' [also known as the fight or flight response] is one of the most important things [leaders] can do."[30] The more intense the threat response, the fewer cognitive resources we have for good, clear thinking. So, leaders must create a non-threatening environment to enable growth, starting with themselves.

Imagine the psychological safety for everyone that is created when leaders are operating at their best—the access to clarity, the perspective, and the ability to provide insight-generating feedback. Yet, in reality, there are times when all of us are not our best selves. In these moments, we lose access to EQ and get stuck in a fixed mindset.

Moreover, at the lower states of the Mood Elevator, we can unwittingly threaten the psychological safety and growth mindset of those we lead. The ideal approach to navigating the lower mood states is to recognize the potential negative effect of words and actions when we are not at our best and minimize our impact.

Curiosity, positioned at the center of the model, is the critical juncture of progression. Curiosity and learning are central to a growth mindset and are among the core tenets of agility in our META model. They are pathways to our most effective leadership moments. When leaders have an individual growth mindset and promote the psychological safety it requires, they are most likely to create the conditions where their executive teams can learn through dialogue, challenge, support, and feedback. When those executive teams embody psychological safety and bring it to how they operate, it flows into and throughout the organization.

A critical part of this is the frequency of appreciation and feedback that people receive from their leaders. Giving appreciation and both positive and constructive feedback on results is important, but so is giving feedback on effort, the contributions individuals made, and how they improved. This creates a culture with momentum, where people feel valued for what they do and how they do it.

One CFO in a telecom organization pointed out in an early conversation that he had experienced a number of "culture interventions" with limited results and consequently did not believe in embarking on a culture-shaping journey. His reputation was as a hard-driving leader with limited empathy, always known to ask difficult questions. This leader was aware that people were wary of him, and while he acknowledged that this style of leadership had its limitations, he didn't know how else to get results. During an offsite "unfreezing" session with his CEO and the executive team, this CFO experienced a significant personal insight about the way his leadership had impacted an event negatively. He profoundly recognized that his low moods had affected those around him. This breakthrough enabled him to develop a different style and approach to leadership with great success. He became a visible leader and champion for culture and passionately supported the culture-shaping journey.

He recognized the power of the shadow of the leader and the role that leaders have in promoting accountability, among other concepts, every day to be the right kind of role model. At his retirement event, we asked him what advice he would give to any leader who was embarking on a significant culture-shaping process.

He said that there were two things that mattered to him, beyond approaching the process in a systematic and robust manner. The first is that the organization needs to know and to keep being told how much this matters to the CEO and the executive team. The second is to strengthen the shadow that every leader casts and to never let up in the quest to bring the best version of themselves to work every day in order to give people and teams the best opportunity to thrive.

Our work has shown there is a high correlation between organizations where people feel valued and appreciated and a growth mindset.[31] The impact is evident in accelerating innovation, the creation of learning organizations, and high levels of accountability and performance.

Proximus: Sustaining a growth mindset

A great example of this symbiotic relationship is Proximus, a Belgian telecoms company. By 2014, the company had positioned itself strategically into essential markets, such as entertainment, but had allowed the business to become static, with a focus on paying its dividend and keeping the government and the unions happy. On its 2014 trajectory, Proximus would be out of cash within five years.

A mandate for growth was led by the Executive Team, which generated an ambitious strategy called "Fit for Growth." Early on, they recognized that the organization had forgotten how to grow: the challenge was to promote growth in an environment with a strong fixed mindset and legacy beliefs.

An essential part of the "Fit for Growth" strategy was the "Good to Gold" culture. This put culture front and center for the delivery of the strategy. Proximus defined its purpose and tied it strongly to the brand

and strategy of the business. "Good to Gold" had a strong focus on creating vitality. The final piece was how to unlock the growth mindset. The values of the organization were rooted in how they defined it: agility, accountability, and collaboration.

The Executive Team decided to increase the engagement and inclusion of the leaders of the company by radically changing the way the annual budgeting process was completed. In the past, leaders would put together their plans and submit them to the Executive Team, only to be told they needed to, for example, take 15% out or to reduce investments or headcount to fit in with the budget that had already been decided. They agreed to a total available budget and allocated it to a number of key strategic priorities that they called "blue chips." The Executive Team assigned a team of senior leaders to each blue chip and tasked them with creating the activity, consistent with the budget, that supported its successful implementation. These were to be submitted to the Executive Team for approval.

That level of freedom was unprecedented. People didn't know how to react. They had been told what to do for such a long time that the requirement to make their own decisions was very different and uncomfortable. The day this process was announced became known as "Black Tuesday" because the organization went into a spasm of indecision.

Within a few days, it was clear that the Executive Team was serious about this, so a few leaders began to explore the possibilities. The effect was extraordinary. Leaders gathered their teams around them to make their own choices as to how their part of the business should be supported. The requirement—and trust in them—to make their own decisions created a sense of energy that could be felt throughout the business within a very short time. Running in the background was a strong commitment by the Executive Team to model the need for praise and feedback that would promote the growth mindset. Many people were waiting for the old coercive behavior to re-emerge so that the naysayers could say, "I told you so." That didn't happen, which fostered a sense of safety in leaders at all levels and generated confidence.

Proximus reached its growth target in less than twelve months, some six months earlier than promised, and continued to grow in terms of customer numbers, top line, and EBIT. The "Good to Gold" culture provided a very different experience for people, and the sense of engagement took the company to a very different place, both as a business and as a place to work. The organization became a very different place to work and there was a palpable sense of positive energy that could be felt walking into a Proximus building. The quality of the leadership shown lay at the heart of the transition.

Some years later, a senior executive from Proximus said that the company had experienced an amazing journey with spectacular results. The cornerstone of that journey was the focus on the culture of the business.

Getting started

The research on the significant positive impact of a growth mindset on leader impact and effectiveness at the leader, team, and organization-wide levels is irrefutable. However, the question remains: how do you unfreeze people across the organization and get started?

The power of a shared experience that brings to life an organization's purpose and provides a taste of the culture at its best can have far-reaching impact. In organizations of diverse sizes and industries, we have successfully employed a shared experience model designed to unfreeze mindsets and engineer insights to pave the way for a growth mindset. The experience itself serves as a psychological anchor for leaders and becomes a ritual of culture. That brings together leaders and teams across the organization to build an aligned understanding of how to work together and a common language that is the foundation for the culture.

This is typically facilitated as an experiential workshop covering a series of concepts and using an "inside-out" methodology that gets beneath the surface to address thought habits, unconscious habits, beliefs, and behavior patterns. Each module in the experience typically begins with an activity that generates an "aha" moment about a key topic (e.g., accountability, teamwork, agility, curiosity, the human operating system). Following is an opportunity for reflection on implications for individuals and the team. The experience incorporates both individual and team commitments to apply insights constructively toward creating a more effective team culture and fostering greater ownership by leaders.

Key takeaways

- Recognize that personal change, starting with your own, is the prerequisite for a healthy culture.

- Creating a culture that can adapt is key. Leaders will create a safer psychological space for people to develop growth mindsets.

- Insight and reflection will make unfreezing mindsets and behaviors easier. Insights will become a self-generating source of positive momentum, influencing the way your organizational culture embraces customers' and employees' changing needs.

Reflections

- How would you describe your capacity for personal change? What impact has it had on your leadership?

- What mindset is holding you back?

- What mindsets are holding your teams back?

- What is the one personal change you are most committed to in order to bring your best to your organization?

- Leaders and teams fail to make a conscious effort to integrate their learnings into their day-to-day activity.

- The organization sees the process as an HR initiative rather than as something that is critical to the future of the business, meaning that the CEO and senior executives can be lukewarm and not recognize their accountability in successfully shaping culture.

All of these reasons, and many more, can be generalized as the lack of a compelling case for culture change, the absence of leader commitment to intentional, lasting change, or both.

Tell a story everyone understands

The core of shaping culture is a simple, commonsense story that generates a deep level of insight and understanding of not only *what* to do, but also *how* to do it. Broad engagement is best generated by introducing a new common language of culture throughout the organization.

That common language needs to consist of simple sound bites that resonate with the definition of the desired culture and that underpin the values. These sound bites create a common understanding of what people mean by collaboration, accountability, or positive attitudes towards change.

Language and memorable stories have meaning for people at both an intellectual and an emotional level. Just as Satya Nadella's blog, which we described in chapter three, explores how Microsoft's purpose and values come to life for the public, those same stories must be told in more detail to build broad engagement internally. It's akin to organization lore being shared around a virtual firepit.

The story can't be complicated. Far too many organizations create clever and complex stories about capabilities and behaviors that are just too difficult to understand, let alone put into practice. If people are being asked to let go of lifetime habits and start to behave in a way that may feel unusual and potentially uncomfortable, they must fully connect with the reasons behind a culture change.

A common language and shared stories provide the means for people to share personal experience through a common medium. This helps build the psychological safety described in the last chapter at scale. It is particularly powerful when working across geographies and dealing with different national languages.

Here, it's important to note the power of teams. Most people interact with their organizations primarily through their teams. When intact teams work together to understand the new story, they build common ground and help to embed cultural mindsets and behaviors in the everyday moments that can develop different kinds of relationships. Generating energy and momentum in teams becomes the engine room for people working differently and is where personal insights are put into practice.

Communicate to drive connection

Broad engagement requires organizations to connect the dots for every employee and every stakeholder among all of the critical elements that sustain an organization: culture, strategy, leadership, employee value proposition, customer experience, corporate social-responsibility strategy, and the day-to-day messages that fill the inbox of every employee. Every organization will have a unique case for change. But there are a number of themes we have observed that consistently engage the entire organization:

benefit of that company's "High-Performance Culture" initiative. One aspect of the company's transformation journey was a significant business restructuring. The leadership teams of one business area were asked to put forward proposals on the restructuring. The executive recalled the following:

> At first, we started down the expected path of turf war behaviors. Surprisingly, however, the shared language created during the "High-Performance Culture" process allowed a small group of more "enlightened leaders" to embrace a bigger team perspective, and they encouraged individuals to be committed to the success of the overall outcome, not just their own part of it. The results were that the change happened quickly, with more alignment and far less resistance than anybody expected. The story of the way that team overcame the challenge became a role model for others to emulate as it was so successful.

The core of the issue was a strong legacy mindset of mistrust and of each business unit keeping that little bit of extra inventory just in case it was ever needed. The increased collaboration and trust led directly to releasing £500 million that had been locked up in the supply chain and to a significant increase in on-time delivery.

This was a significant moment, which other teams began to notice. Over a period of time, the rest of the organization wanted to know what had changed in the supply chain. Within two years, the rest of Rolls-Royce had engaged in "High-Performance

Culture" workshops, which now underpin their global culture. These sessions enabled participants to experience engineered epiphanies that brought to life the company's values and the core tenets of its high-performance culture, as exemplified in its motto, "trusted to deliver excellence, act with integrity, and operate safely." The company has also invited its suppliers to become a part of the same process, with some success, because it creates such a valuable foundation for all work. This didn't happen by accident: there's a carefully designed set of processes and activities that deliberately supports this self-sustaining cultural ecosystem.

The journey started in 2010 and has gone through three distinct phases. Its high-performance culture has successfully enabled the organization to foster innovation, integrate acquisitions, inspire and engage employees at all levels, and accelerate alignment and onboarding of new employees, leaders, and partners. The culture journey was launched with a clear line of sight to Rolls-Royce business drivers to secure lasting impact.

CEO Warren East served as the chief culture officer. (See chapter six for more on why this was important.) Senior leaders of each supply chain unit (SCU) at Rolls-Royce enhanced their capabilities to play prominent lead roles in the culture-shaping journey. A well-defined governance structure and appropriate culture lead roles have allowed Rolls-Royce to build a critical mass of champions, facilitators, and sponsors across every part of the business. Each SCU has evolved and maintained culture-shaping work plans, and each has refreshed these as part of the overall annual planning cycle, ensuring continued systemic alignment of culture and structure (see chapter six). Culture action teams have promoted two-way communication channels to support the execution of integration plans within HR, communications, measurement, and training and development.

The culture effort at Rolls-Royce has demonstrated impact and success for a decade, measured through business results such as freeing up cash, engaging employees, and accelerating business strategy. This was a particular victory for Rolls-Royce because some senior leaders started out dubious.

Key takeaways

- Culture becomes real and meaningful to employees across the organization when action and commitment are visible and authentic.

- Broad engagement happens when an intentional, clear plan for action and a culture communications strategy connect the culture through every message throughout the organization.

- Employees bring their whole selves to work every day when they are inspired and engaged. Shared language and shared experiences help to unfreeze mindsets and build common ground for a strong culture.

- An inspiring and engaging employee experience leads to a successful customer experience.

- Strong purpose and values become the compass point for organizations. In times of crisis, this compass point can inspire agility, clarity, and action.

Reflections

- How are your culture and values demonstrated through visible action in your organization and among employees?

- How has your organization's purpose enabled you to weather the COVID-19 crisis and emerge stronger? What have you learned through the crisis that you want to embed for the *future*?

- How has your organization intentionally shaped culture and engaged all employees?

Chapter six

Pulling all the levers for systemic alignment and accountability

To describe the success of DBS, the Singapore-based bank, Piyush Gupta, its Group CEO, cites its "pervasive culture":

DBS has been successful in our digital transformation over the years because of a pervasive culture of experimentation, agility, and innovation.[35]

The bank has earned multiple "best bank in the world" titles over the years, from publications including *Euromoney*, *The Banker*, and *Global Finance*. It is widely cited as being in the vanguard in terms of embedding digitization across the full range of banking processes and services, leading to its growing strength and influence on the financial landscape throughout Asia and the world.

This accomplishment was a result of a digital transformation journey that began under the stewardship of Gupta, who joined the bank in 2009. DBS laid out a bold strategy to perform at a global level, improve the internal culture, and, most importantly, to excel in customer service. The strategy set the foundation for the bank to adopt digitization, which centered on "Making Banking

Joyful" for the customer. This would be achieved through three strategic initiatives: to become digital to the core; to be customer-obsessed by leveraging customer journeys that focused on making the bank invisible to the customer; and to create a start-up culture (in a company of 33,000 employees) to encourage experimentation, innovation, and calculated risk-taking.

DBS created the following "ABCDE" as its core story:

- A – Have a hairy **audacious** goal.

- B – **Build** on talent and develop people (most senior hires are now internal).

- C – The secret sauce is the DBS **culture**.

- D – Have **discipline** in execution across the whole organization.

- E – **Employees** are the core of success. Encourage employees to embrace a growth mindset, enable every individual to become a better version of themselves, empowering them to drive change to make a positive impact on others.

The fact that the senior leadership team consistently pushed for change meant that they became critical role models and that change was not perceived as a fad. To prevent change from appearing daunting to individuals, the bank encouraged employees to learn and adopt new ways of working together by making it social through a myriad of activities such as hackathons, team competitions, and learning festivals, as well as an extensive list of learning materials and programs to instill confidence and a growth mindset. Over time, everyone became deeply immersed in the digital transformation and took ownership of the process.

Employees became empowered to make more agile decisions, such as frontline staff being able to deal with issues in the moment, rather than referring to their leaders to improve customer experience. The bank eliminated 250,000 hours of time customers spent that added no value to them, making the company more convenient and less visible to its customers (banking through smartphones, not branches) and allowing it to offer better service.

DBS has based this success on an evolution of the purpose of the two banks from which it was created—the Development Bank of Singapore and People's Bank respectively—into its current purpose: the inspiring goal to "create impact beyond banking." DBS links performance-management behaviors that support the purpose and values to salary and promotion. It also regularly monitors engagement, the degree to which employees are living the values, and management effectiveness, all of which have allowed DBS to track the transformation process.

DBS has accelerated its ability to expand existing businesses and new engines of growth, drive its sustainability agenda, and redefine the future of work.

Aligning culture and structure

DBS's pervasive commitment to its culture journey was directly linked to its strategic ambition of digital transformation. All four of the key principles for a thriving culture were in place, beginning with purposeful leadership, a full commitment from the leadership team to take up the mantle of personal change, a focus on building broad engagement around the culture through a drumbeat communications effort, and consistent reinforcement of that engagement.

What DBS exemplifies particularly well, however, is systematic alignment of all strategic systems and processes—from HR systems to customer-experience processes—to their "PRIDE" values ("Purpose-driven, Relationship-led, Innovative, Decisive, and Everything fun") with its culture. This allowed them to assess the true impact of culture change with tangible metrics, such as the elimination of non-valuable customer time, and to enjoy the intangible impact of empowered decision-making. The next chapter will delve more deeply into the range of culture metrics that leaders can use; here, we will explore further how to develop the same level of systemic alignment.

What systemic alignment fundamentally requires is hardwiring the culture into the structure of the organization. Connecting organizational levers to cultural tenets ensures there are no unintended disconnections at the organizational level, in the same way that leaders living the culture prevents the "do as I say, not as I do" failures of culture-shaping. For example, DBS promotes the value of being "relationship-led," which focuses on building long-lasting relationships and strong teams by collaborating widely and working together. But if its compensation system rewarded individual performance more significantly than collaboration, it would create the unintended consequence of encouraging employees to demonstrate a more individualistic attitude. Instead, its compensation and HR systems strongly support the value of collaboration.

The roots of our culture-shaping methodology have historically stressed the importance of aligning strategy, structure, and culture. We focused in earlier chapters on aligning culture and strategy in support of organizational purpose. (Our recent survey of 500 CEOs suggests that companies see better cultural and financial results when they start in this order.[36]) Organizational structure is typically driven by the business model. Leaders ask whether they are supporting an integrated business model, a holding company model, or a regional business model and whether a matrixed, decentralized, or centralized structure will work best to create clarity of direction and decision rights, as well as a commitment to cultural goals.

Aligning culture with those key organizational levers that sustain or thwart an organization's cultural goals is less straightforward. It's necessary to create alignment with all levers, from organization design and capabilities to operational excellence and customer processes. Leaders must determine whether culture and structure are aligned by asking questions such as: How do we attract and hire employees? How do we develop and retain them? How do we design the entire employee life cycle? How do we ensure our brand delivers on the promised customer experience? How do we foster simplicity across the organization? How do rewards and recognition drive the right employee mindsets and behaviors?

It is crucial for leaders to understand that functions responsible for specific systems and processes, such as HR, cannot drive alignment alone. All hands are required to properly weave culture throughout the fabric of the organization, starting, as always, at the top. While systemic alignment is about the hard stuff, when an organization successfully weaves the hard stuff and the soft stuff together, its culture can thrive beyond leadership changes, beyond market changes, beyond policy changes, and even beyond crises and disruptions like COVID-19.

Accountability

Systemic alignment is not possible without accountability. CEOs, executive leadership teams, and culture leadership teams each take on different areas of accountability. All require the balance of a high level of human touch with intentional discipline and rigor.

The CEO as chief culture officer

Ultimately, by default or design, it is the CEO whose shadow most impacts the culture and who owns the culture-shaping journey. The CEO leads the process and signals the veracity of the commitment in his or her words and actions.

In our survey of 500 CEOs around the world, 82% said they had focused on culture as a priority in the past three years, though only 26% saw it as a top-three influence on financial performance. Those with the most cultural and financial success focused on both internal and external relationships. These leaders, more often than other CEOs, said that collaboration and trust were not only important, but also were prevalent in their company culture. And 100% of the culture connectors CEOs in the study took personal accountability for living the culture.[37]

The executive leadership team

But CEOs don't act alone. Their impact is enhanced or diminished in many ways by the effectiveness of their leadership teams. Given that systemic alignment is an all-hands-on-deck proposition, these leaders must take equal responsibility for modeling and driving the culture in their functions and lines of business.

This group of leaders sets an example that is more personally visible to the wider organization. What this team promotes is essential, but equally important is what this team permits. In our work, we see that the most common barrier to successful culture-shaping is when the behavior of some leaders who do not live the values is overlooked because of their strong financial contribution to the organization. When executive teams permit their peers to behave that way, the commitment and credibility of the whole team—and the whole culture—fall into question.

Executive teams also typically oversee, sponsor, and support the culture road map that methodically aligns cultural tenets to every facet of the organization. They maintain a line of sight to what is helping or hindering the process and bring the road map credibility as senior stewards who act objectively and in the best interest of the organization.

The culture leadership team

A CEO and executive team who hand-select an enthusiastic and influential team of line leaders to play a critical role in sustaining culture will see strong benefits. A culture leadership team can oversee and manage the nuts and bolts of the culture-shaping journey and implementation. Their remit is both to accelerate progress and to address unanticipated organizational roadblocks. They can dive into organizational knitting to understand real-time applications of new culture values and to observe dynamic forces so that they can take fast action to amend or address problems as needed. For example, we have seen such teams identify disconnections between culture goals and the compensation system, highlight a need to align performance management with culture, ensure the content and tone of employee communication is supportive of broad engagement (see chapter five), and note when decisions are made and acted upon in ways counter to the culture.

Culture leadership teams are typically responsible for the following:

- Ensuring that the culture-shaping process becomes the vehicle to drive well-defined progress in supporting the strategy, instead of being driven by one-off events

- Making sure that the best people are engaged in implementing the culture road map and have the time and resources to do so

- Eliminating barriers to progress as they are identified

- Overseeing all workstreams connected to the process

- Communicating with the executive team on progress and support needed

Culture leadership teams work best when they accomplish the following:

- Model the identified culture of the organization

- Ensure that everyone is working for the benefit of the organization as a whole and not for their own sliver of it

- Share accountability in decision-making for the greater good of the organization

- Include relevant stakeholders at appropriate times, and invite new ones where necessary

- Focus effort where the business need is greatest

Mutual of Omaha: Lasting alignment from top to bottom

James T. Blackledge has led Mutual of Omaha as president since 2014, was appointed CEO in 2015, and chairman of the board in 2018. Under his leadership, the company has engaged in an intentional culture-shaping effort, building on its 100-year legacy. Branded "Mutually Connected," the company values, supporting attributes, behaviors, and beliefs connect Mutual associates with a common vision: "For every customer—a financial future imagined, planned and secured." The "Mutually Connected" values—"We Exist for Our Customers," "We Act with Integrity," "We are Innovative," "We are Accountable for Results," and "Together We Achieve Greatness"—are owned and lived by the executive team and have been integrated into every aspect of the organization's infrastructure. They are placed at the center of all HR processes and are leveraged to drive change, from the integration of IT systems to the creation of a new company brand. The culture leadership team plays a prominent role in refreshing the culture journey while internal facilitators and culture champions maintain a steady connection to the values and culture year over year.

In addition to a balanced scorecard of business performance metrics, talent metrics are key to demonstrating how Mutual of Omaha's culture continues to move the needle on performance. Year-over-year revenue from 2017 to 2020 showed steady growth, resulting in record revenue in 2020. Annual review of their culture has provided evidence of a continued upward shift in engagement and perceived cultural strength. After six years, the journey continues today as leaders demonstrate the requisite agility to adapt to market and disruptive forces.

Key takeaways

- Culture requires an intentional, agile path to integrate cultural tenets into every thread of the fabric of an organization.

- Without full integration into systems and processes, cultural messages and values may be at odds with the rewarded behaviors and outcomes.

- A CEO serves as the chief culture officer, by design or by default, and will either accelerate a culture and its impact or miss the opportunity to accelerate the pace of strategy execution.

- At all levels of the organization, the culture requires leadership, champions, and facilitators to support, reinforce, and challenge the alignment of cultural values with the day-to-day experience of employees and customers.

Reflections

- Where are you on your culture-shaping journey? What is your next leap, and what will it require?

- Does your CEO and your organization operate as a culture accelerator? If so, what are examples of positive impact? If not, what holds you back?

- Considering the integration of cultural tenets and values into the fabric of your organization, which systems and processes are the priority?

Chapter seven

Building a road map to improve culture metrics— and financial metrics

The primary ambition behind the "The Power of One," Helen of Troy's transformational cultural journey, was all about taking the organization to the next level in order to achieve step-level growth.

Built on more than 50 years of history with impressive results, the consumer-products conglomerate grew by acquisition, was highly dispersed in terms of geography, encompassed many different businesses, and therefore was siloed and not aligned in terms of culture. With little collaboration and limited financial incentive to work together, the company had lots of opportunity for improvement. Guided by the purposeful leadership of CEO Julien Mininberg, as part of his broader, multi-year transformation plan, he and a strongly committed leadership team embarked on an ambitious journey to transform its culture and take its results to the next level. The goal was to move from good to great, as Mininberg described in the following way:

> We knew that we had to unify, empower, and engage our people 100% and bring them together. That was not a natural act inside of Helen of Troy. It required us to overhaul the organization and the people systems.

As we embarked on an intentional culture journey we named "The Power of One," we brought together our top leaders to inspire and engage them in participating in the transformation. At the same time, working to rebrand the company, we brought to life the idea that we are boldly bringing brands into a family powered by exceptional people. Together, we are elevating lives, [and] soaring together, and the mantra emerged—"We are Helen of Troy."[38]

With a clear, compelling organizational purpose—"Elevating lives, soaring together"—CEO Julien Mininberg and a hand-picked team of top performers representing several departments, levels, and geographic regions defined their core values: "I RISE."

- **I**n touch: We're deeply connected with each other, customers, consumers, shareholders, and our communities.

- Mutual **R**espect: We treat each other with integrity, professionalism, and transparency.

- **I**ntegrity: We're constantly ideating and finding new ways to improve our products and processes.

- **S**hared Success: Together, we achieve what none of us can do alone.

- **E**xceptional people: Our people feel and act like passionate owners. Their experience and skills build our business and nurture the people around them.

In addition to painting a clear vision of the future and inviting employees at all levels to participate in bringing the culture to life, the company added a reward and recognition idea to ensure that every employee would feel and act like an owner of the company. Mininberg's engagement with every employee came through in a pivotal action that took engagement to the next level: "In 2018, we issued transformation shares to every employee in the company, right down to the person that pushes a broom and up to the people who run large parts of the company. The share grants went to people of one day's tenure and people of 40 years' tenure. It didn't matter which location, which division, or which job responsibility—50 shares all around. Those transformation shares were game-changers. People didn't just act like owners; they literally are owners."

In the four years since embarking on its culture shaping journey under the Power of One, business performance at Helen of Troy has accelerated markedly, as have most of the other performance metrics it tracks. Revenues grew by more than 40% from fiscal year 2018 to fiscal year 2021, and adjusted earnings per share grew by more than 60% during that same period. In its most recent fiscal year, Helen of Troy crossed a major sales milestone to achieve $2 billion in sales. Ever consistent with the people-first culture at Helen of Troy, CEO Julien Mininberg issued a second round of transformation shares in 2021 to associates around the world, again to all levels, tenures, and locations. Their results and their greatly increased engagement speak loudly across all metrics, including the company's stock performance. At the start of the company's transformation journey in 2014, the company stock price had averaged $60/share and its market capitalization was about $1.5 billion. In 2018, the year in which the company issued its first grant of 50 shares of stock to its associates, the average price per share was $108. As the culture and other transformation initiatives continued to bear fruit, the average price in 2020 rose to $185 per share. As of this writing, in September of 2021, its stock is trading in the $230s, and its market capitalization is nearly $6 billion.

Helen of Troy tracks several key metrics to understand the health of its culture and how it impacts performance. The company has seen its retention scores rise, especially among top performers, who are staying, growing, and developing long-term careers. On the recruiting side, it has increasingly become an employer of choice. The company frequently promotes from within, and when it fills positions from the outside, the land rate for first-choice candidates has risen by more than 20 percentage points in recent years. On Glassdoor, a popular independent rating site, Helen of Troy has also shown marked improvement, rising from a 2-3 star company in 2016 to 4.5 stars in 2021, best in class among the peer companies it tracks. Its net promoter score, which Glassdoor calls "recommend to a friend", is at 94%, and its CEO approval rating is at 99%. Helen of Troy also surveys employees from time to time using our Corporate Culture Profile (see appendix), and has seen its scores rise on all 28 of the survey's metrics each time, even during the pandemic. Helen of Troy is very proud of how powerful its culture transformation has been, helping its associates come together, fully engage, and drive the company to new heights.

Where do you stand today?

The most effective culture journeys we have observed start with the end in mind. That's as true of metrics as of cultural characteristics. Leaders should undertake any culture journey with the understanding that culture is a continuum and by recognizing where they are on it. A survey like our Corporate Culture Profile can help leaders understand how employees at all levels, in all functions and regions, feel about the culture and how it is, or is not, positively affecting financial performance. By visualizing a culture journey against the inflection points from level to level, it is easier to plan intentional interventions, apply the four principles, anticipate challenges, and avoid the risk of culture complacency.

The culture continuum

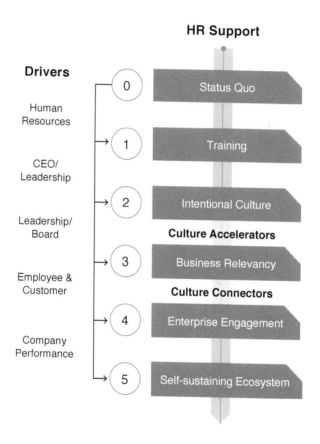

Level 0: The status quo is good enough.

At this level, company values are articulated in the employee handbook but don't reflect the reality of how people interact or how they are hired, promoted, or recognized. Culture isn't referenced in strategic discussions, and leaders are not intentionally supporting culture as a priority aimed at advancing strategy and performance. The company's mission, vision, purpose, values, and behaviors are not systemically aligned with the organization and are not measured. There is inconsistency in how the values support the business and how leaders live the values. Expectations and practices are in conflict; for example, employees are urged to move faster and take ownership, yet multiple approvals and micromanagement slow them down.

Level 1: We need to educate ourselves about culture.

At this level, executives and employees acknowledge that culture matters, but it still appears to be supported in voice only. Company values are discussed during onboarding but aren't really lived in daily interactions. Leaders express different levels of commitment to culture, from open skepticism, to being curious, to being all-in. When leaders communicate, values are woven into the message content, tone, and manner—but there are no coordinated communications to create a deeper understanding of what the values mean and how they should drive behaviors. Instead, actions and policies are instituted to address frustrations. For example, a policy forbidding cell phones in meetings is put in place to fix the underlying problem of people being disengaged or not fully present. When negative behaviors emerge, more employee surveys are done. Culture is measured by changes in specific limiting behaviors, not outcomes. Culture is primarily addressed through training programs. Style dominates over substance.

Level 2: Our culture should be intentional, and as leaders, we should drive.

Culture matters to the organization, and leaders want to improve it. Culture is visible: values are highlighted in meetings, recognized in company communications, displayed on conference room walls, and incorporated in meetings, large and small. Most employees know them well. A common language around the culture has been communicated and is being reinforced from top levels to the front line (although not all leaders live the values as consistently as they speak about them). A growing feeling of openness and opportunity is increasing employee feedback and suggestions. Successes are celebrated. Values and behaviors are beginning to be integrated into performance reviews.

Level 3: Culture is connected to results.

In our recent survey, a group of CEOs emerged as culture accelerators. These leaders tied culture to performance as a business imperative and as a strategic asset. More broadly at this level, the factors that influence employee engagement are clearly defined and aligned to customer outcomes. Cultural strengths, gaps, and specific initiatives are addressed during the strategic planning process. (These kinds of efforts are important steps toward CEOs becoming successful culture accelerators.) A spirit of continuous improvement permeates the company, fueled by strong vision, purpose, and values. A business case connecting positive culture results to improved business outcomes is in development, drawing on data-driven insights and analytics.

Level 4: We engage at the enterprise level: our employees' experience is our customers' experience.

Culture has moved from being an initiative to being a strategy that influences business outcomes. A strong focus on a people-centric culture inspires and engages employees, who in turn improve the customer experience. The results are increased customer satisfaction, enhanced loyalty, and bottom-line sales growth—proven through real-time measurement and ongoing reporting. Technology is leveraged to foster and capture two-way feedback, measure engagement, and build stronger relationships. An increase in suggestions from employees leads to more streamlined customer service and better products conceived through a more dynamic, inclusive development process. The executive dashboard measures engagement and the impact it has on market share, margin, and revenue growth, among other outcomes.

Level 5: Culture is a self-sustaining ecosystem and a core strategic asset.

The culture is embedded (consciously and unconsciously) in the company's DNA. There is clear alignment, transparency, and empowerment in support of a company's mission, vision, values, and behaviors. All voices are heard, and employees clearly understand their roles and their connection to the company's direction. Employees feel valued and supported by peers, direct leadership, and the executive team. There is a disciplined, closed-loop feedback process that focuses on actions and outcomes. Analytics are used to move from insight and understanding to foresight and proactive planning, allowing leaders to stay abreast of changes in the competitive landscape and adjust strategy, structure, and culture with greater agility.

The road map

Getting to culture as a self-sustaining ecosystem requires an intentional and methodical road map that is informed by thoughtful planning and executed with discipline and rigor. As former Yum! Brands CEO David Novak says, "It's heartwiring and hardwiring. Culture has to be both."

An effective road map for culture creates an explicit connection between the desired culture, the business strategy, and the performance imperatives for the organization. Applying a future-focused lens, the planning process requires a look at tomorrow's strategic climate, followed by assessment of the current strengths, weaknesses, opportunities, and threats that may affect execution of the business strategy. Then, with that strategic context in mind, leaders can consider the strengths and gaps of their current culture. This reflection is usually supported by data from an employee survey.

At this point, leaders can begin a practical discussion about systemic alignment: How do we need to change to commit ourselves to a thriving culture? What is the case for culture and the inspiring narrative and communications required for a drumbeat of engagement? How will we engage both hearts and minds to support broad engagement of all employees? Considering the need to hardwire the culture, which initiatives, systems, and processes are priorities? How will culture be measured within a balanced scorecard of human capital and business metrics?

Ultimately the enterprise culture road map will accomplish the following:

- Align senior stakeholders around the full scope and impact of a focus on shifting culture

- Provide a clear line of sight for leaders between the "as is" and "to be" cultures

- Identify critical integration points, metrics, and milestones to link culture to business priorities and performance

- Ensure the sustainability of an intentional culture journey through meaningful reinforcement and governance

Leaders must also remember, however, that this road map cannot be static. Shifts happen in the external and internal environment that require mid-course corrections and adjustments. Lines of communication and flow of information require continued attention and reinforcement to apply and adjust the culture as needed. With an agile approach informed by strategic analysis and the kinds of culture metrics described in the rest of this chapter, the culture road map becomes a living document to point the way toward a thriving culture for the long term.

A dashboard for culture impact

An organization's case for culture lays out why culture matters and why it is being actively shaped now. In the case of Helen of Troy, the case was rooted in an ambitious goal to take the company to the next level of performance and growth. Julien Mininberg described a number of initiatives that were in play at the height of the transformation and which offered a clear scorecard of metrics to determine progress. For Helen of Troy the tangible metrics included the following:

Human capital metrics

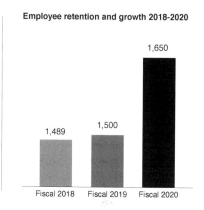

Improvement on CCP Essential Drivers

From 2018-2020, the CCP scores on all the essential dimensions showed statistically significant improvement:

Customer quality and focus	7.4
Ethics and Integrity	11.0
Positive Spirit/ Vitality	9.0
Direction/ Purpose	16.2
Agility/ Innovation/ Growth	9.3
Appreciation/ Recognition	11.4
Collaboration and Trust	12.0

Employee retention and growth 2018-2020

- Fiscal 2018: 1,489
- Fiscal 2019: 1,500
- Fiscal 2020: 1,650

These metrics relate directly to Helen of Troy's transformation agenda and its culture journey. Leaders celebrate progress and address barriers to ensure positive momentum. The scorecard is simple and clear, metrics are observable and measurable. In addition to viewing quarterly metrics, the organization assesses the culture annually against the baseline. Taken together, these metrics provide a valuable lens for the culture journey, linking both human capital and business performance metrics as evidence of culture's impact in the organization.

Other companies will benefit from the same sort of balanced-scorecard metrics that are integrated into a dashboard and that show how the organization is progressing or not progressing on the total journey. This requires addressing both the visible and the invisible.

A fundamental approach to metrics for "the hard stuff" at the enterprise level starts with structure and form, materials, and systems and processes. The methods and routines that enable day-to-day activity are measured in dollars, time, and resources and are monitored to generate improvements that fine-tune the business and the customer experience.

A human-centered, talent-based approach articulates "the soft stuff." Competencies and desirable behaviors are defined and made explicit through frameworks that include credos, performance standards, and balanced scorecards. These frameworks are frequently used to focus on the tangible value that competencies, organizational values, and behaviors have on influencing employees to do the right thing, to clarify targets, to create the constructive competition, and to enable results-based compensation. They can also assess invisible factors, such as the degree of psychological safety employees feel, their overall engagement, and their sense of inclusion.

As with Helen of Troy, most leaders will find that a mix of these two, with some culture-specific indicators, is the right way to measure culture impact.

Real-time updates

Given the pace of disruption today, leaders need frequent updates on how their organization is performing and feeling, whether they are just embarking on a culture journey or are far along the path to a self-sustaining culture. Frequent digital pulse and crowd-sourced input can provide an instantaneous view of current employee perception and sentiment and can inform individual employees about how their view compares to peers. With artificial intelligence, such digital conversations bring aggregate themes and sentiment to the top of the conversation chain and enable participants to feel supported or challenged by the prevailing view in real time. Further analysis of the data resulting from crowd-sourced conversations can provide deeper understanding of how the needle is or isn't moving on cultural drivers. These digital pulse surveys have become even more critical now that employees are engaging virtually and workforces are operating in a mix of remote, in-person, and hybrid environments.

The immediacy of feedback and two-way vehicle of digital conversations was critically important to a professional services firm that wanted to understand the impact of virtual work on employee engagement in order to gauge the potential of a long-term remote model. A monthly pulse survey over a 10-month period revealed an increasingly strong desire for remote work, reports of higher levels of performance, and improved work-life balance.

Putting metrics together

There is great truth to the adage that "what gets measured gets done." When it comes to the metrics that will give you hard data about your performance and your culture, your business and your people, declaring your cultural ambition and defining your starting point are key. We regularly employ four approaches to culture assessment:

- **The pulse of the culture today:** The current snapshot from crowd-sourcing instruments that promote digital conversations and engagement

- **The essential drivers of successful culture:** The degree to which relationship and performance drivers form a cultural foundation, measured by instruments like the Corporate Culture Profile

- **The culture's ability to accelerate strategy execution:** An organization's ability to mobilize, execute, and transform with agility, measured by an instrument like the Organization Acceleration Questionnaire (see appendix) that assesses both the hardwired elements and the mindsets and behaviors of the organization

- **Leadership shadow:** Purposeful leadership is required not just at the start of the culture journey, but throughout it. Leaders need feedback, and employing a multi-rater instrument mapped to values is a useful measure of the impact that leader commitment and behaviors are having on their team and on the company as a whole. The Leadership Acceleration Questionnaire is a tool that can assess how a leader mobilizes, accelerates, and transforms with agility and how the values are lived

A truly integrated view of culture metrics takes the tangible—what you can see—and the intangible—what you can't see—into account. In summary, depending on the maturity of the organization, we look at four cultural metrics to help define a complete and integrated view of progress on a culture journey.

Key takeaways

- An organization's case for culture will affect which metrics matter most in defining progress and impact, and so belong on the organization's balanced metrics scorecard.

- Culture metrics include tangible metrics related to human capital impact, as well as intangible metrics that influence psychological safety and fitness for individuals, teams and the organization overall.

- Determining a culture baseline, grounded in data and research, is foundational to setting the road map for a culture-shaping journey.

- Digital pulse checks—monthly, for example—provide an immediate understanding of current employee perception and sentiment and can serve as a vehicle for two-way communication and immediate insight for participants.

Reflections

- Considering your organization's case for culture, which metrics matter most?

- What human capital and performance metrics would be most relevant to track? Do you track them, and how? How often?

- How would you rate the degree of psychological safety and fitness in your organization? What actions are required to move the needle?

Chapter eight

Inspiring thriving cultures in the "new now"

Darin Harris became CEO of Jack in the Box, a U.S. fast-food chain, in June of 2020. He described his start this way:

> In my first six weeks as CEO, I have witnessed the nimbleness and passion within this brand. I am proud of the way our franchisees, the teams in our restaurants, our employees, and our partners have responded swiftly to the changing occasions of our consumers amidst the pandemic . . . I am excited about taking the learnings from this uncertain time and using them to fuel the remaining part of 2020, as well as our strategy into 2021.[39]

Jack in the Box franchises more than 2,220 restaurants in 21 states. It pioneered both the all-day breakfast and the late-night category and has a reputation for serving crave-able foods with a smile and a spirit of fun. Ninety days into his tenure, Harris had yet to meet with his team in person due to the limitations of the pandemic environment and the remote work mandate in California. Yet he wanted to tap into the strengths of the organization to ensure an agile response to the volatile market.

At the top of his priority list were culture, strategy, fostering a growth mindset amongst leaders, and creating a fresh start with key stakeholders, including franchisees. Harris was intentional and consistent in virtual team sessions, and his leadership shadow quickly emerged, with servant leadership at its core. He engaged team members to imagine a set of cultural values that would inspire the organization's commitment to each other, to franchisees, to partners, and to guests. He said, "We need to serve others well by putting them before ourselves without expecting anything in return."

Culture in an unexpected present

As we described in the preface and chapter one, even before the dramatic events of early 2020, there were strong signals that organizations were starting to think differently about what companies exist to do, shifting from shareholder capitalism to stakeholder capitalism. The events of 2020 accelerated this process and, among many other consequences, will define the future of work for the foreseeable future.

Many companies are shifting to greater home working, developing models that halve their office space, moving to flexible hubs out of major cities, and fully supporting hybrid ways of working.[40] All this has had and will continue to have a huge impact on employees, organizations, and, of course, cultures.

Leaders now understand their cultures in the context of having emerged from a period of unprecedented change and needing to continue to adapt and reshape in order to thrive. Many leaders have been increasing their focus on the health and well-being of employees throughout, a focus which is often founded on organizational values and purpose. Many organizations that had not yet intentionally focused on culture came through the crucible of 2020 understanding the value of connecting their organization, their employees, and other stakeholders by uncovering their organization's innate purpose and values.

As in other crises, we often saw people show up at their best to overcome adversity: pulling together, supporting employees, and demonstrating a desire to create a sense of psychological safety for everyone. Leaders and teams put huge efforts into redesigning work, reallocating resources, and bringing the technology needed to run teams and organizations virtually quickly up to speed. Humanity has risen to the fore: all of us have, at some point, seen our team members and colleagues in their home environments, with children running into rooms and cats walking across laptops. This has created a very different dynamic that, particularly in the early days, strengthened cultural values such as trust and resilience.

However, organizations and cultures must continue to adapt if they are to continue to thrive in an increasingly virtual world.

Tactics to maintain a thriving culture in the "new now"

The good news is that our survey of 500 CEOs around the world showed little difference in the share of employees mostly or entirely engaged in applying their cultural values in their day-to-day work, whether the workforce is working mostly in person (77%) or in a more fluid, hybrid working model (73%). But it is also clear that with change and prolonged crisis, fatigue sets in. At the time of writing, many leaders are deeply concerned about the long-term effects of hybrid workplaces on most aspects of their organizations, not least on the health of the culture.

Where to start to address those concerns? The notions of "going back to work" or "getting back to normal" are still common among leaders, especially following such an extended period of virtual and remote work practices. Where there is uncertainty among leaders and their teams, there is a call for clarity and confidence. Where there is disruption, there is a need for rhythms and consistent practices of connectivity. Where there is exhaustion and a blurring of personal and work time, there is a need for clear policies and supportive leadership practices to enable employees to find their balance even when working in relative isolation. Where there is resistance to go back to any prior semblance of normal and the advantages of flexibility and working from home outweigh the challenges, there is a call for leaders to listen, to understand, and to acknowledge employee voices and feelings.

To do all of this, leaders need to consider their own leadership shadows. As with the start of a crisis, moving toward the end presents an important moment for dialogue and understanding. To show empathy, personal change is required from leaders who may, for example, feel more strongly about a return to the office than employees. Clear and concrete actions connected to employee input that are communicated consistently will build broad engagement. Executives have taken actions such as declaring "Zoom-free Fridays" or "meeting-less Mondays" and are adopting digital communication approaches aimed at minimizing the complexity of overflowing in-boxes and maximizing the immediacy of communication made possible with collaborative tools.

More broadly, this "new now" has reinforced the importance of the shadow of the leader and of purposeful leadership as the foundation of a thriving culture. Leaders need to find their own clarity and confidence that their organizations will succeed. We recommend six actions to CEOs and leadership teams as they reassess the culture road maps based on the compasses they need now:

- **Look forward.** Stop looking for a "timeline for return" and instead ask: "What will it take for our company to be successful in this environment in the near term and in the long term?"

- **Be open and transparent and reinforce purpose and values.** Continuously ask for input and clearly communicate to employees about what you are hearing in the context of your organization's purpose and values. Create opportunities to listen and demonstrate empathy. Be open about your own feelings; don't be afraid to show vulnerability.

- **Celebrate the milestones that reinforce the best of the culture.** Understand and plan to mark key milestones with collective celebration to give employees a sense of forward progress. Promotions are a great example of such a milestone.

- **Shift language from "returning to work" to "the future of our work."** This recognizes that there will not be a snap back to the past and emphasizes a future focus, applying lessons learned. The emergence of the hybrid meeting has changed the way that people connect remotely; no longer do people have to be the disembodied voice on a poorly connected phone. Improved technology and remote participation have changed the agendas and the design of meetings.

- **Enable differentiated "future of work" strategies** as a way to stand out from competitors. Many companies have differentiated their "future of work" experience through creative approaches to collaboration, using virtual reality spaces as a replacement for the water cooler; implementing digital apps and nudge technology for community and connection; embedding purpose through volunteerism and community engagement, which also serve as regular meet-up experiences; and implementing unique teamwork rhythms and rituals that strengthen a sense of belonging, e.g., "Mindfulness Mondays." The key is for these "future of work" practices to be authentic to the culture and the employee experience.

- **Foster confidence, consistency, and resilience** by developing "future of work" policies, practices, and patterns. Ensure that leaders are balancing one-on-one touchpoints with team interactions. Be purposeful about meeting agendas and sensitive to the amount of internal screen time.

Yet, even leaders who accomplish all of this will still face the reality that there are many factors out of our control. We all need to be ready to make tough decisions, pivot quickly, and act decisively—in other words, to be agile. Agility is essential both to manage the immediate priorities of today and to remain future-focused.[41]

Another important starting point in terms of culture is to maintain regular digital pulse surveys throughout the organization (see chapter seven) to really understand how people feel and how they view internal and external environments. In the current context, it's more important than ever to regularly take a look in the mirror. It allows leaders and organizations to focus on the themes that are most critical to their organization's culture, as well as to understand which things they wish to consign to history.

Applying the four principles in the "new now"

The above tactics are an important starting point in keeping cultures afloat. Leaders will also benefit from stepping back to the four core principles of culture-shaping—with some fresh considerations—as they work to support their cultures and update the enterprise culture road map.

Purposeful leadership

- Ensure clarity about the role of leaders in defining and reinforcing the organization's purpose and living into its values. This will require intention, focus, and a discipline that wasn't required when leaders could lead by walking around.

- Build a deep understanding of the current state of the organization, how it has changed, and how it will continue to evolve. Continually assess what new ways of working, mindsets, and behaviors are required.

- Connect organizational purpose, which is central to helping companies thrive, to employees' and customers' renewed attention to their own purpose in life. Use purpose as a binding force for remote or hybrid organizations.

- Ask what new rituals and practices will maintain alignment and connection among the top leadership team.

Personal change

- Ask if the current values will be able to sustain their future after the test of 2020. Revisit them, reshape them, but, above all, recommit to them on a personal level, recognizing that this may require personal change.

- Be agile, committed to a growth mindset, and attuned to changes in the market, customer demands, and, most importantly, the lives and communities of employees.

- Explore what changes leaders themselves should make and what changes they can inspire across the organization to support broad resilience and agility.

- Seek to maintain the benefits of the more inclusive, more human leaders and organizations that most have become. Preserve that connection while seeking ways to build inclusion in a hybrid environment.

- Lean into vulnerability in order to navigate the discomfort of uncertainty and the socially and political challenging environments to which organizations are still adapting. Acknowledge that while individually, leaders won't have all or even many of the answers, collectively, leaders and teams leaning on organizational values will discover them.

Broad engagement

- Be intentional, clear, and creative about creating two-way channels, communicating with authenticity, and ensuring leaders are ready to deliver communications that are just-in-time, yet meaningful, as culture continues to be a lifeline.

- Make the best and most creative use of technologies that support interactivity, facilitate dialogue and connection, and create a common experience to maintain the drumbeat of culture.

- Set a clear definition of the employee experience and provide reasons why employees should want to be engaged. Rely on your organizational purpose, bring it to life, and tie it to the day-to-day lives of employees right now. In navigating community-based crises, bring that purpose to life for employees and stakeholders.

- Let customers' new expectations be the guide, as they are now often as remote as employees. Understand what will make their lives easier now, and empower employees to deliver it.

Systemic alignment

- Take the time to design new ways of working that will be essential for the organization's success. Review all human capital systems and practices to ensure that these will enable the culture to continue to thrive and to sustain new ways of working that are fit for today's purpose.

- Make the recruitment and onboarding processes as engaging and effective as possible. As new employees, even new CEOs, are hired and onboarded in remote circumstances, this will cement their future success.

- Desired mindsets and behaviors should be part of performance reviews, and, in a hybrid world, it's more important than ever that they not be perfunctory. In the "new now," it is vital that these conversations are grounded in empathy, clarity, and organizational values.

- Refresh your road map for culture. Identify the critical touchpoints and integration opportunities that will ensure that employees are living, breathing, and experiencing the culture from their homes, offices, and remote locations. Engage senior leaders and re-engage a culture leadership team.

Key takeaways

- Periods of crisis and disruption require steady, transparent and future-focused leadership. Through authentic communications, leaders can break through uncertainty with immediate actions that can stabilize the organization and reassure employees.

- Such times, more than any other, also require empathetic leadership and the ability to listen with understanding in order to secure psychological safety and provide a safe place for employees to voice concerns.

- The shadow of the leader plays a critical role in fostering agility, resilience, and clarity.

- Communication is oxygen for organizations at all times, but most especially in times of crisis. Leaders who communicate openly, honestly, vulnerably, and consistently will enable employees to weather uncertainty and move to action.

Reflections

- How can learnings from crises like the pandemic inform new ways of working for your organization? What do you want to retain from the experience and integrate into the fabric of your culture?

- What positive leader behaviors that emerged during the pandemic do you wish to see institutionalized? Which less productive behaviors emerged that you believe the culture should not support?

- With the four principles as a guide, what is your action plan going forward?

Chapter nine

Shaping a future-focused culture in your organization

Given all the fundamental changes facing organizations today and the rapid pace of those changes, there is ever-more agreement among leaders that purpose-driven, future-focused cultures are at the core of thriving organizations. A culture pointed toward a clearly defined purpose will weatherproof an organization and ensure it can mobilize, execute, and transform with agility, no matter the challenge.

Learning from culture accelerators

We have noted some findings of our CEO survey throughout this book. Taken together, they offer several striking insights as you set out on the next steps on your culture journey:[42]

- While most CEOs made culture a priority, most are not intentional in their pursuit of culture as a driver of financial performance, even when they try to be. As we described in chapter seven, metrics matter, and developing a culture without a clear connection to impact and to financial performance is like searching for gold and then hiding it in the hills.

- The companies in our survey that were led by culture accelerator CEOs have financial performance (assessed by a three-year revenue CAGR) that is more than double that of other companies surveyed. Culture accelerator CEOs link culture to strategy (including using tactics such as those described in chapter seven) and then demonstrate purposeful, intentional leadership in forming cultures that correlate with impact, specifically with financial performance. They put people first and build broad engagement.

- Culture accelerator CEOs focus their efforts on the aspects of culture which they believe have the most positive impact on financial performance more often than others. These CEOs focus in on two critical aspects of culture that create a positive effect: collaboration and trust, and customer and quality focus. It's notable that, more often than other CEOs we surveyed, culture accelerators go beyond just saying that collaboration and trust are important; they say those qualities are prevalent in their own cultures and reinforce them by communicating them internally and externally. They enable an enhanced customer experience and support good relationships with external stakeholders. This focus on broad stakeholder engagement aligns with the overall greater focus on organizational purpose that we have noted.

Even culture accelerators can't succeed alone

It does take a village to shape a culture and sustain it. While the CEO plays a critically important role as culture accelerator, they cannot shape culture alone. Not one of our exemplar CEOs did so. From reliance on the senior team, to broad engagement of the entire organization, to systemic alignment with human resources, operational excellence, and every other corporate function, shaping a thriving culture required an all-hands-on-deck approach. It is irrefutable that the CEO must be committed and engaged every step of the way and must intentionally inspire and engage others. It is also critical that the CEO be surrounded by a village of purposeful leaders and culture carriers from across the organization.

Mapping your road

To become the leader of a thriving company that makes the most of its investments in culture, developing a clear road map for the organization's culture-shaping journey is critical. We have provided you with several tools that can assist in assessing where you are, what your desired destination or next cultural milestone is, and what steps you need to take to get there. We'll close by bringing those back together with a simple approach to initiating a road map.

Gather a team of purposeful leaders—perhaps the executive leadership team (ELT), a culture leadership team, or a group of ELT members along with high-potential leaders. Be thoughtful and intentional about convening a team who can take action to meaningfully impact the culture while maintaining momentum and focus.

Then engage in the discussion on the following pages, which we hope will give you an opportunity to apply the lessons from our exemplars and practically put into practice the four principles.

Start with the end in mind

What does success look like at the end of Year 1, Year 2, Year 3, and beyond for your organization's strategy? What metrics will you have moved the needle on?

_____

_____

_____

_____

_____

Determine strategy, structure, culture alignment

Considering the alignment of strategy, structure, and culture, define the following:

Strategy, structure, culture

ALIGNMENT

Purpose

Why We Exist
- Impact on the world

Strategy

Business Direction
- Strategy, vision, mission
- Value proposition
- Competitive advantage

Structure

Organization Capability
- Talent - competencies
- Organization design
- Systems and processes

Culture

Norms of Behaviors
- Collective habits
- Shared values
- Conditional beliefs

Current and future strategic priorities:

_____

_____

_____

_____

_____

Structural considerations (operating model, decentralized versus centralized, and other relevant changes in structure):

_____

_____

_____

_____

_____

The culture continuum

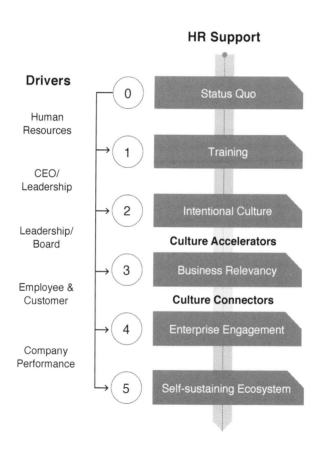

Where are you on the culture continuum? What is the next level you hope to achieve? What potential barriers do you need to address?

_____

_____

_____

_____

_____

Current culture tenets and the shifts required to deliver on the future strategic imperative (mission, purpose, vision, values, etc.):

_____

_____

_____

_____

_____

Assess the four principles in your organization and where you stand today

Four principles

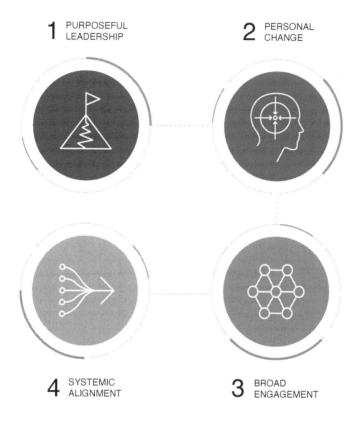

1 PURPOSEFUL LEADERSHIP

2 PERSONAL CHANGE

4 SYSTEMIC ALIGNMENT

3 BROAD ENGAGEMENT

How do you see purposeful leadership present in the current environment? Identify the top two strengths and the top two gaps.

_____

_____

_____

_____

_____

On a scale of one to five, how would you rate the level of personal change and commitment you see from top leaders in the organization? Where is an increase in personal change and commitment needed most?

_____

_____

_____

_____

_____

From a broad engagement perspective, what is working well? What needs to be improved? How would you define the employee experience? Is the culture clearly being reinforced?

_____

_____

_____

_____

_____

Considering the hardwiring and systemic alignment of the culture, where is the culture most established? Where are there gaps? (Consider performance management, the compensation system, leadership capability and development, quality and safety metrics, etc.)

_____

_____

_____

_____

_____

Define the metrics that matter for you

What financial performance metrics do you most need to impact through culture?

_____

_____

_____

_____

_____

What other human capital, customer, quality and/or safety metrics does the culture need to impact?

_____

_____

_____

_____

_____

Set the baseline

What recent survey data do you have to establish a current baseline for your culture? Where is the culture strong today? What opportunities to improve are evident? What is the impact of these strengths and opportunities on the business today?

_____

_____

_____

_____

_____

What overall strengths of your cultural journey have you uncovered? What gap areas do you need to address?

_____

_____

_____

_____

_____

Take the first steps

This exercise may have opened up a meaningful dialogue among leaders, it may have illustrated that you are operating as a culture accelerator CEO, or it may have revealed that you are part of the "village" successfully accelerating the culture journey in your organization. Whatever it sparked, the answers can help you shape your own intentional, purposeful, consistent focus on shaping culture, which is absolutely essential to shaping an organization's future.

"Future-focused" is about impact on employees, customers, and stakeholders. And it is about performance today as well as the foreseeable tomorrows. It requires leaders to look around the corner, maintain a watchful eye on change, prepare for the unexpected, and navigate uncertainty with clarity of vision, purpose, and a commitment to shaping a culture that will inspire every employee to thrive and will successfully deliver the desired future. Stay future-focused: shape your culture and you will shape your future.

Afterword: Pioneering the field of corporate culture

Dr. Larry Senn

Enabling thriving cultures has never been more important than it is today. At this moment in time, the shadow that leaders cast is the greatest determinant of organizational health, employee well-being, and fulfillment of company purpose. Culture is indeed at a tipping point in our world.

The road to my discovery of how to systematically shape a culture was long and winding. I started my career with an engineering degree and an MBA. The words "corporate culture" didn't exist in 1960, and business schools taught a very mechanistic view of leadership. My first job was in an aerospace company. It sounded like a glamorous and interesting job from the outside, but I ended up hating it. It was hierarchical, bureaucratic, territorial, and, for me, stifling. I didn't know it then, nor did the aerospace firm, but I quit because of the CULTURE.

With the help of one of my UCLA professors and another student of his, Jim Delaney, I then founded Senn Delaney Management Consultants as a process improvement firm. My path to 50 years of fascination with culture began as I started to do consulting work with a variety of companies. To my surprise, I found that most organizations were like dysfunctional families. They had trust issues, turf issues, hidden agendas, politics, resistance to change, hierarchy, and bureaucracy. I was struck by how easy it was to get results in some organizations and how it was virtually impossible in others.

History was written in more ways than one when a guy named Sam at a relatively small company called Walmart had a vision of bringing low-cost goods to rural America. He was going to change the retail game by taking costs out of moving goods from the manufacturer to the customer and by having "happy boxes" with greeters.

Sam was like an evangelist. He preached the virtue of his vision, and people got on board with his higher purpose. Delaney and I were invited as consultants to be part of a team that revolutionized the Walmart supply chain. It was a different organizational experience than we had ever had. Everyone on the team was working for a greater good. They were open to trying totally different ways of doing things. There was a special "can-do" attitude. Team members were innovative, collaborative, accountable, trusting, transparent, and fully engaged. The results were remarkable and deeply fulfilling.

We then tried to do similar work in the supply chain at another retailer, Woolworth, and it was a complete failure. The reason was obvious. They had none of the qualities we experienced with Sam at Walmart. They were resistant to change and bureaucratic, and the only purpose I could see they had was to maintain the status quo. It struck me that, while the two were relatively similar organizations, Woolworth was likely to die and Walmart would likely become a major player in retailing, all due to invisible qualities no one talked about or wrote about at the time.

The Walmart–Woolworth experiences, and others like them, led me to conclude that organizations were like people, each with its own personality and set of beliefs and habits. I wondered, where did this unique personality come from? What role did it play in the success of organizations?

In my search to understand this phenomenon, I came across a professor at USC who had written a paper on "organizational character." He said he had been looking for a doctoral student to research the topic. That led to my dissertation, which turned out to be the world's first field research on organizational culture.

Of the many findings from my research, two were most notable. The first is that, over time, organizations become "shadows of their leaders." They take on the beliefs and attributes of their leaders, both good and bad. The second important finding was influenced by the work of an early social scientist, Kurt Lewin, who said, "When we are young, we are like a flowing river—and then we freeze." We start out in life open and curious, and then get frozen in our habits. Lewin believed unfreezing through deeper insights was required for true behavior change. That led me to begin to design team trainings with "engineered epiphanies" that could powerfully "unfreeze" old habits of leaders and make way for new ways of behaving and thinking.

The findings from the dissertation became the core of the work we have done for over 50 years. I realized that if we could enable leaders, especially CEO teams, to behave in ways that cast the right shadow, both culture and performance would be impacted. I also understood that the way to get adults to change was not by telling them to change but through insight-based team training. Those "aha" moments from engineered epiphanies could unlock habits and create new insights and possibilities for leaders and organizations. These two elements—the shadow of the leader and engaging the entire organization in insight learning about critical culture concepts—became the cornerstones of the early work of Senn Delaney.

Who would have believed more than 50 years ago that the world would one day recognize culture as the greatest driver of a company's success? Today, the fact that culture has significant impact on performance seems clearly understood, but there is still a gap in understanding what it really takes to change historic habits and create a culture that ensures an organization's future.

We grew into a global consulting firm that has worked on culture with hundreds of CEO teams and their organizations in more than 40 countries and in 15 languages. Along the way, we attracted some amazing purpose-driven people who joined the firm to make a difference in the lives of people through culture.

To broaden the capabilities we could offer clients and to expand our reach, we were delighted to join Heidrick & Struggles in 2013. Senn Delaney is now an integral part of Heidrick Consulting as its center of excellence on culture. In *Future-Focused*, Rose and Ian share our latest research and findings on the power of culture. They bring it to life through stories and examples of inspiring CEOs and exceptional cultures. I am grateful for the exemplars in this book who have inspired us and our work. I am confident that you, too, have been inspired and informed by their stories.

This book is the result of the collective experience of so many generous and knowledgeable people, both clients and colleagues. The wisdom shown and gained over many years has provided the perspective that appears in the preceding pages.

We would like to highlight the contributions of the CEOs who offered their experience as exemplars of how to put culture front and center in the delivery of their strategy. We would also like to offer appreciation to Krishnan Rajagopalan, the Heidrick & Struggles president and CEO, who has lent his sponsorship and support to this project at this critical moment for leadership and culture. Dr. Larry Senn is acknowledged as the "father of culture," and we cannot overstate the impact and influence he has had on the work that we do in this space.

Andrew LeSueur and the global leadership team of Heidrick Consulting have been engaged and supportive of this process, as have the teams of people in our offices around the world who interact with clients every day. We thank you all for the amazing work that you do, both in visible client delivery and in the less visible engine of delivery that runs in the background.

We are fortunate to work with team members across Heidrick Consulting who are committed to enabling a world better led. In direct and indirect ways, every one of our colleagues has contributed to this book. While we can't acknowledge everyone, special appreciation goes to colleagues, past and present, who worked with our CEO exemplars and led many of the engagements that formed the culture success stories throughout the book. From Partners to Principals, Engagement Leaders, Client Service Team Members and Senior Consultants, the passion and dedication each have brought to our clients have inspired countless thriving cultures.

We would also like to thank our colleagues in Executive Search for their partnership, insights, and dedication to enabling a better-led world. Our collective passion and dedication to our clients as "One Heidrick Team" has equipped us to foster thriving cultures and to support purposeful leaders around the globe.

Thanks also must go to Josselyn Simpson, who took our words and crafted them into this form that we are proud to publish. We are also grateful for the talents of Paul Diniakos in bringing to life the graphics throughout the book.

Finally, we offer our heartfelt thanks to Melissa Wilson and Julie Anixter for their wisdom and support throughout the writing of this book.

Appendix

Heidrick & Struggles uses two primary organizational assessment tools, the Corporate Culture Profile (CCP) and Organization Acceleration Questionnaire (OAQ). Although they both measure an organization's performance, each tool has a slightly different focus and uses a different data set to correlate its results. Each has its place and application, as we describe below.

The Corporate Culture Profile (CCP)

Heidrick Consulting's Corporate Culture Profile™ (CCP) is a well-established and validated measurement tool used to assess the culture within an organization. It is derived from survey data and interviews with more than 150,000 leaders in their respective organizations over a 30-year period.

The overall profile page shows an example of a client in 2019. These are average ratings converted to a 100-point scale. Scores below 60 are in the red, which is considered a danger zone since such characteristics are very likely to be cultural barriers to high performance. Scores of 85 points and above are in the green, which indicates the presence of "healthy, high-performance" characteristics. Those in between—in the yellow—mean "caution—needs some additional attention."

The corporate culture profile

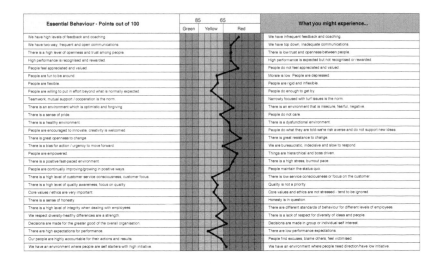

Essential Behaviour - Points out of 100	85 Green	65 Yellow	Red	What you might experience...
We have high levels of feedback and coaching				We have infrequent feedback and coaching
We have two-way, frequent and open communications				We have top down, inadequate communications
There is a high level of openness and trust among people				There is low trust and openness between people
High performance is recognised and rewarded				High performance is expected but not recognised or rewarded
People feel appreciated and valued				People do not feel appreciated and valued
People are fun to be around				Morale is low. People are depressed
People are flexible				People are rigid and inflexible
People are willing to put in effort beyond what is normally expected				People do enough to get by
Teamwork, mutual support / cooperation is the norm				Narrowly focused with turf issues is the norm
There is an environment which is optimistic and forgiving				There is an environment that is insecure, fearful, negative
There is a sense of pride				People do not care
There is a healthy environment				There is a dysfunctional environment
People are encouraged to innovate, creativity is welcomed				People do what they are told-we're risk averse and do not support new ideas
There is great openness to change				There is great resistance to change
There is a bias for action / urgency to move forward				We are bureaucratic, indecisive and slow to respond
People are empowered				Things are hierarchical and boss driven
There is a positive fast-paced environment				There is a high stress, burnout pace
People are continually improving/growing in positive ways				People maintain the status quo
There is a high level of customer service consciousness, customer focus				There is low service consciousness or focus on the customer
There is a high level of quality awareness, focus on quality				Quality is not a priority
Core values / ethics are very important				Core values and ethics are not stressed - tend to be ignored
There is a sense of honesty				Honesty is in question
There is a high level of integrity when dealing with employees				There are different standards of behaviour for different levels of employees
We respect diversity-healthy differences are a strength				There is a lack of respect for diversity of ideas and people
Decisions are made for the greater good of the overall organisation				Decisions are made in group or individual self interest
There are high expectations for performance				There are low performance expectations
Our people are highly accountable for their actions and results				People find excuses, blame others, feel victimised
We have an environment where people are self starters with high initiative				We have an environment where people need direction/have low initiative

This particular organization, for example, had grown complacent over many years and was lacking in innovation. It found itself in a market that was being heavily disrupted. The CCP highlighted its need for a specific focus on several characteristics that were holding back performance and creating some significant burnout in its employees. The leaders were expecting people to give high levels of discretionary effort in a results-driven environment. But day to day, people experienced, among many other factors, a lack of appreciation for their effort and skill, resulting in their not feeling valued. This dynamic was storing up trouble for the future, and the CCP pinpointed the issue.

The CCP is underpinned by the eight essential dimensions of culture, listed in chapter two.

The diagram below of the essential dimensions for the company above highlights their need to redefine their purpose, become more focused on the engagement of their people, encourage greater agility and innovation, and promote a growth mindset.

The essential dimensions

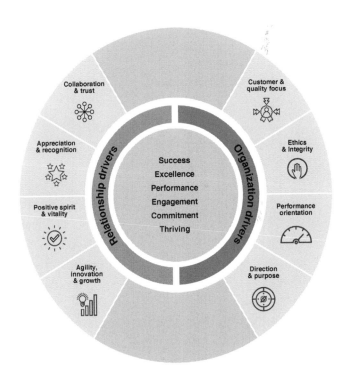

This information, combined with the data in the CCP, allowed the senior leaders to understand better where the biggest levers for change were in their culture. This became the focus for a robust process that was given credibility by the CEO's belief in the power of culture to transform the performance of that business.

Key features of the CCP survey:

- The essential drivers and behaviors have been validated, tested, and derived from the analysis of more than 150,000 data points sourced from 160+ organizations.

- It takes only 15–20 minutes to complete the online survey.

- There is no limit to the number of people who can take the survey in an organization.

- The survey provides participating organizations with a significant capability to compare the cultures of teams and businesses across its organization.

- The data provided can be split in many ways—for example, by country, by line of business, by level of leadership, etc. This provides a significant opportunity for benchmarking.

- Progress on commitments can be monitored through repeating the CCP.

- It can be delivered in several languages: English, French, German, Italian, Spanish, Portuguese, Dutch, Flemish, Czech, Finnish, Russian, Mandarin, Traditional Chinese, Indonesian (Bahasan), Japanese, Korean, and Thai.

The Organization Acceleration Questionnaire (OAQ)

Heidrick & Struggles developed the Organization Acceleration Questionnaire (OAQ) based on extensive research with FT500 companies.

We have found, through this research, that the success of an organization requires a focused and structured acceleration program based on careful analysis that leads to removing barriers and drag factors while taking dynamic steps that will drive and accelerate overall performance.

Our research revealed 13 drive factors that accelerate performance. We also found that FT500 companies that were able to mobilize, execute, and transform with agility (META) while leveraging the 13 drive factors generated nine times the average compound annual growth rate of others. Individual organizations' degree of acceleration is assessed through employee surveys. We use parallel surveys to assess degrees of leadership acceleration, team acceleration, and board acceleration.

META framework

The 13 drive factors give a detailed perspective and help to pinpoint what is helping a given organization accelerate. It gives a comprehensive view on the ways that often complex elements of an organization's makeup can be complementary or can be interfering with each other.

OAQ drive factors

Mobilize	Customer First	Always responsive to changing customer demands, low customer attrition, consistent service excellence
	Energizing Leadership	High-energy buzz, empowerment at every level, strong role models who inspire others to bring their best performance
	Clarity	Everyone aligned and committed to purpose, ambition, and clear priorities

Execute	Simplicity	No bureaucracy, lean processes, streamlined structure
	Ownership	Meritocracy, delivery culture, integrity-driven processes
	Winning Capabilities	Talent magnet, great talent development processes, best talent in key roles

Transform	Innovation	Culture of disruptive thinking, ideas generation and experimentation, fast adoption
	Challenge	Supportive, frank feedback and debate, highest performance expectations
	Collaboration	Work as one organization, high level of trust, joined-up processes and communication

Agility	Foresight	Think ahead to anticipate and plan for changing circumstances
	Learning	Learn quickly to avoid repeating the same mistakes and continuously improve
	Adaptability	Quick to adapt to changing circumstances
	Resilience	Recover quickly and emerge stronger from setbacks

The OAQ also measures 13 drag factors, which gives organizations perspective on what is holding them back so they can create a balanced view of themselves, taking into account the push and pull of activities and opinions.

The results enable leaders to take a hard look in the mirror to assess their current ability to accelerate, from which point they can begin a targeted journey of organizational improvement or transformation.

OAQ drag factors

Mobilize	Internal Focus	Chronic service failures, high customer attrition, overtaken by market disruptions
	Fatigue	KPIs on red, key projects delayed, disengagement
	Confusion	Unclear purpose and strategy, lack of focus, too many conflicting priorities

Execute	Complexity	Too many layers, unjustified process variation, complicated metrics
	Unclear Accountability	Overlapping accountabilities, reward effort not impact, victim mentality
	Skills Gap	Weak talent pipelines, losing the best people, avoid tough people decisions

Transform	Fear	Missed value opportunities, stagnation, outdated products and services
	Complacency	Acceptance of mediocrity, taking too long to remove poor performers, avoid straight talking
	Competition	Silos and politics, distrust, hoard information

Agility	Hindsight	Always looking at the past for answers to current problems
	Immunity	Liability to learn from mistakes; avoids failing at all costs
	Inflexibility	Slow to adapt to changing circumstances
	Frailty	Unable to recover from setbacks; weakened by them

Key features of the OAQ:

- The questionnaire can be completed by the entire organization, senior leaders, or a representative sample of the organization.

- It is online and secure, with individual access links.

- It takes approximately 20 minutes to complete.

- Companies can track progress by retaking the survey over time.

- It provides data that can be used to benchmark teams within the same organization.

- It is available in several languages, including English, Chinese, Vietnamese, Khmer, Hungarian, Tamil, Slovak, Turkish, Italian, German, Portuguese (Brazilian), Portuguese (European), Spanish (European), Spanish (Latin American), French, and French Canadian.

Notes

30. David Rock, "Neuroscience hacks you can use to change behavior," *Science of Success* podcast, September 26, 2019, successpodcast.com.

31. Ian Johnston, "Creating a growth mindset," *Strategic HR Review*, Vol. 16, Issue 4, pp. 155-160.

Chapter five

32. Tom Peters, "next five minutes," blog, https://tompeters.com/quote/13378/.

33. https://www.ariedegeus.com/.

34. Rose Gailey, Ian Johnston, and Andrew LeSueur, *Aligning Culture with the Bottom Line: How Companies Can Accelerate Progress*, Heidrick & Struggles, heidrick.com.

Chapter six

35. DBS, "DBS clinches global accolade for innovation in digital banking," August 2, 2021, prnewswire.com.

36. Rose Gailey, Ian Johnston, and Andrew LeSueur, *Aligning Culture with the Bottom Line: How Companies Can Accelerate Progress*, Heidrick & Struggles, heidrick.com.

37. Rose Gailey, Ian Johnston, and Andrew LeSueur, *Aligning Culture with the Bottom Line: How Companies Can Accelerate Progress*, Heidrick & Struggles, heidrick.com.

Chapter seven

38. Julien Mininberg, "The Power of One: Helen of Troy's culture transformation journey," interview, Heidrick & Struggles, heidrick.com.

39. "Jack in the Box Inc. reports third quarter FY 2020 earnings; reinstates quarterly cash dividend," Jack in the Box, August 5, 2020, jackinthebox.com.

40. For more insights on these topics, see Yulia Barnakova and Steven Krupp, "The future is now: How leaders can seize this moment to build thriving organizations," Heidrick & Struggles, heidrick.com. See also Yulia Barnakova, Nedra Johnson, and Andrew Jakubowski, "Digital inclusion: Five considerations for leaders to build on gains and avoid pitfalls in the hybrid world of work," Heidrick & Struggles, heidrick.com.

41. For more on agility, see Becky Hogan and Steven Krupp, "Agility for the long term," Heidrick & Struggles, heidrick.com.

Chapter nine

42. Rose Gailey, Ian Johnston, and Andrew LeSueur, *Aligning Culture with the Bottom Line: How Companies Can Accelerate Progress*, Heidrick & Struggles, on heidrick.com.

Index

hybrid work. *See* remote work

innovation: 80, 93

insight: 57, 69, 83

    individual: 56

    leading to behavior changes: 59

    leading to culture shifts: 56

    need for: 60

intangible factors. *See* invisible factors

invisible factors: 114, 117

Jack in the Box: 120–121

James, LeBron: 50

"jaws of culture, the": 16

journey, culture-shaping: 37, 67–69, 76, 95, 98

    and CEOs, 100; financial benefits of: 69

    failure of: 77–78

Kelleher, Herb: 15–16, 26

Kelly, Gary: 26

King, Rollin: 26

leader: as role model: 66

    nurturing change: 82

    personal change of: 32, 57, 60

    role of: 60. *See also* commitment of leader

leadership: 9

    purposeful: 30, 43, 49, 82, 126

learning: 65

learning, work-based: 56

Lewin, Kurt: 148

living the culture: 76, 97

living the purpose: 60

Lumen: 74–76

M&A (mergers and acquisitions). *See* mergers

Meggitt: 44–46

mergers: 19, 21, 44, 74, 80

merging cultures: 21, 74

    failure of: 20

surveys: digital pulse: 115–116, 125
    of employees: 30, 115–116
systemic alignment: 33, 82, 95–97, 112, 128–129, 136.
    See also alignment tangible factors; *See* invisible factors
teams, importance of: 79, 134
Thomson Reuters: 22
Trust Barometer: 15
unfreezing: 69. *See also* habits
utilitarianism, modern: 57
values: 12–13
    examples of: 37, 67, 88, 92, 95, 100, 104–105
    exemplified by leadership teams: 97
visible factors. *See* invisible factors
Walmart: 147
Wood, Tony: 44–46
Woolworth: 147
workshop: 66, 71, 86
Yum! Brands: 54–55